# Eiger Direct

# Eiger Direct

## The epic battle on the North Face

PETER GILLMAN
AND
DOUGAL HASTON

Vertebrate Publishing, Sheffield
www.v-publishing.co.uk

# Eiger Direct

Peter Gillman and Dougal Haston

 **Vertebrate Publishing**
Omega Court, 352 Cemetery Road, Sheffield S11 8FT, United Kingdom.
www.v-publishing.co.uk

First published in 1966 by Collins, London. This edition first published in 2020
by Vertebrate Publishing.

Front and back cover photographs by Layton Kor and Chris Bonington.
Other photography by Chris Bonington and Peter Gillman.
Eiger route map photograph by Markus Spiske.

This book is a work of non-fiction based on the life, experiences and
recollections of Peter Gillman and Dougal Haston. The author has stated
to the publishers that, except in such minor respects not affecting the
substantial accuracy of the work, the contents of the book are true.

A CIP catalogue record for this book is available from the British Library.

ISBN: 978-1-912560-59-2 (Paperback)
ISBN: 978-1-912560-58-5 (Ebook)

10 9 8 7 6 5 4 3 2 1

www.v-publishing.co.uk

Produced by Vertebrate Publishing.

# Contents

# Introduction to the New Edition

Can it really be fifty-three years? That was my first thought as I contemplated writing an introduction to a new edition of *Eiger Direct*, the book I wrote with Dougal Haston about the dramatic events on the North Face of the Eiger in February and March 1966. Some of my memories are etched as clearly as the face itself when it soared against a scintillating blue sky. Others are blurred and faded, again like the face when – as far more often – it was obscured by the storms which savaged the climbers during their epic battle to reach the summit via a new direct route.

Looking back from the perspective of a lifetime, it is striking to consider how naïve we must appear. Aged twenty-three when the climb started, I was in my second year working as a journalist and also undertaking my first full reporting assignment, as I had been employed at the *Daily Telegraph* weekend magazine as a feature writer. I had grabbed the assignment when I learned that the *Telegraph* was backing the British–American team led by John Harlin and needed a reporter at Kleine Scheidegg. Those were the days when you wrote your reports on a manual typewriter and dictated them to the *Telegraph*'s Fleet Street office by phone – and there was just one phone available at the Kleine Scheidegg hotel, to be found in a cabin in the entrance hall. I would monopolise it for up to half an hour at a time – and then, if possible, occupy it for a further few minutes to talk to my long-suffering wife Leni, at home in south London with our two young children.

Previously I had been reluctant to write about mountaineering, as I was only too aware of how journalists were regarded in the mountaineering world on account of their propensity to sensationalise everything and make endless mistakes. But this opportunity was too good to pass up. It became even more alluring after I had arrived at Kleine Scheidegg and learned that a rival German team was equally intent on making the first direct ascent of the North Face – thus adding the element of a race to the attempt.

Were the climbers themselves naïve? It seems a curious term to apply to those two bands of climbers. The British–American team had the superstars: Harlin, Haston, the Colorado rock expert Layton Kor – and Chris Bonington, at an early stage in his drive to make a living from his passion for climbing, and enlisted by the *Telegraph* as the team photographer, although his role was soon to merge with that of full-on team member. The Germans were, so far as we were concerned, unknowns from the Swabia region of southern Germany. But they came with a self-confidence that we misread at first, unaware as we were of their technical abilities and their fraternal loyalties.

The climbers' struggles were truly heroic: a pitting of their energies against one of the most formidable challenges in mountaineering. The two teams had radically different tactics which converged as the days – and weeks – passed. Yet naïvety could be an appropriate term when considering the two teams' equipment, which now seems hopelessly outmoded: breathable outer clothing had not been invented, winter climbing tools were heavy and primitive, cooking equipment hardly ever worked. These failings were to culminate in the devastating technical mistake which altered the dynamics and the narrative three days before five climbers – four Germans plus Haston – reached the summit in the midst of the most ferocious storm of the whole winter.

So it was that Haston, Bonington, Kor and I returned to Britain after the climb, Bonington and Haston spending long, tedious hours in a hyperbaric oxygen chamber that was considered the most effective therapy for their frostbite (but is now no longer used). That was when we devised this book, where I was to be the principal writer while Haston provided his graphic contributions on handwritten pages which I merged into the manuscript. Bonington, of course, provided the bulk of the photographs, which so vividly captured the dramas on the face: the skill and nerve of the climbers and the extraordinary Wagnerian ending. I wrote quickly, delivering the manuscript to the original publishers, Collins, in about four weeks. The book appeared in the autumn of 1966, followed by overseas editions with a range of titles in the US, France and Japan. It was well reviewed, winning praise for its descriptive qualities, its narrative suspense, and its control of the complex and interlocking events on the face.

There matters rested for almost fifty years. Haston died in a Swiss avalanche in 1977, Kor of cancer in 2013. As the fiftieth anniversary approached, I had an urge to tell the story again. This time I would provide the full backstory of the ascent and the climbers, crucially giving far more space and credit to the eight German climbers (three of whom had since died) who were participants, first as rivals, then as partners, in the ascent. That story, co-authored with Leni, was published as *Extreme Eiger* in 2016. We acquired a precious new friendship, with the family of Peter Haag, the German team co-leader who had died of cancer in 1981.

Even afterwards, however, people would tell me how much they had enjoyed the original tale – and how *Eiger Direct* was all but impossible to obtain, as it had been decades out of print. I read it again, and wondered whether the writing could be considered naïve. In some ways, perhaps, but it has qualities of freshness and immediacy that left me immodestly impressed. It also has the key elements that made the ascent so remarkable: the attempt that became a race, the contest that became an alliance, the tragedy that preceded the triumph. I felt that the mix of reportage and narrative would still appeal, both to those of that era, and to those coming to the story anew. When I discussed the idea of republishing it with Jon Barton, he responded with satisfying alacrity, judging it worthy of inclusion in any back catalogue of classic mountaineering texts. Jon's record as head of the UK's foremost mountain-eering publisher speaks for itself.

Apart from a very few minor factual corrections, the text stands as it did in 1966. It thus contains Harlin's exaggerations about his previous sporting activities which I – naïvely – did not question at the time, but which are revisited in *Extreme Eiger*. I felt that it would be improper to subject the text to major revision, so that it remains as a record of a contemporary perspective on an epochal ascent.

So here it is. As always, dear reader, you must be the final judge.

Peter Gillman
August 2019

# Note on the Text

When Dougal Haston came down from the summit on 26 March 1966 we decided to write a book together. He was obviously the main source for what had happened on the mountain, whereas I knew what had happened at Kleine Scheidegg, where I had been working the radio link between the climbers and the base. As we recorded these conversations on tape, we have been able to recount them with complete accuracy. Because of the technical problems involved in a first-person account by two people, we have written this book in the third person, with the exception of Dougal's account of the summit push, where we felt the first person was more appropriate.

For the benefit of non-climbers we have provided a glossary of technical terms.

Peter Gillman
June 1966

# Acknowledgements

We should like to thank the many people who helped us during the climb and when we wrote the book. The *Weekend* and *Sunday Telegraph*s provided the all-important financial backing for the climb. Various equipment manufacturers, all of whom we mention in the text, were generous to us. Many of the people living and working at Kleine Scheidegg showed us kindness and sympathy. Marilyn Harlin and John Harlin's parents gave us details of John's life, and Marilyn Harlin kindly allowed us to quote from John's writings. The members of our team told us their stories of the climb. Leni Gillman and Clare Wignall helped us with the manuscript.

We should also like to thank the members of the German team for the friendship they showed us during our shared experiences on and below the Eiger.

Dougal Haston and Peter Gillman
June 1966

# Chapter I

The North Wall of the Eiger is the greatest face in the Alps. Like a giant, gaunt tooth it rises a sheer 6,000 feet from the meadows of Alpiglen. At its base it is a mile wide. It is in the front rank of the peaks of the Bernese Oberland, and the huge amphitheatre that forms its upper part attracts the first storm clouds to arrive in the area.

The lowest part of the Face, comprising one-third of the total, is more easily angled than the rest. Then comes a steeper series of tiers of ice broken by rock steps. The Face then steepens even further to the point where almost no ice adheres to it, except for the icefield in the centre of the upper part called the Spider. Radiating from the Spider are snow-filled cracks that form its web.

The Eiger's summit was first reached by an Irishman, Charles Barrington, in 1858. He chose it in preference to the Matterhorn – also unclimbed at the time – because it was nearer to where he was staying. He followed the ridge between the North Face and the West Flank. The Mittelegi Ridge, which runs up almost from Grindelwald and arrives at the summit from the east, was first climbed by a Japanese, Yuko Maki, with three Grindelwald guides in 1921. In 1932 the Swiss climber Dr Hans Lauper, in a party of four, climbed the North-East Face, a fine classical route. Traditional alpinists now considered the problem of the North Face solved. To them, there was no question of venturing on to the vast wilderness of rock and ice to the right of Dr Lauper's line.

But there was a new generation of climbers, out of harmony with classical alpinism. In 1935 two climbers attempted the North Face proper. They were Max Sedlmayer and Karl Mehringer and they came from Munich, home of the new thinking. In three days they reached the top of the vast Second Icefield, about half-way up the Face. Then a shattering storm hit the Face. Sedlmayer and Mehringer took two more days to reach the top of the Flatiron, a huge rock buttress that ends above the Second Icefield, and there they died. The place became known as the Death Bivouac.

At once the two Germans were violently attacked. The Swiss journal *Sport* wrote: 'It is a deeply to be regretted result that the survivors of modern Eastern Alps' technique should now inflict this evil demonstration on Swiss peaks. If they had reached the top it would have been merely a degradation inflicted on one of our great peaks, with the honoured traditions of mountaineering perverted into monkey tricks.'

Colonel E. L. Strutt, President of the British Alpine Club, reprinted the article in the *Alpine Journal*, of which he was the editor. He added the footnote: 'With which sentiments, while expressing sympathy for the relatives of the young climbers, every British mountaineer will concur.'

In 1936 four more climbers from the Eastern Alps, Edi Rainer and Willy Angerer, both Austrians, and Anderl Hinterstoisser and Toni Kurz, Bavarians, made an attempt, joining forces when the two parties met low down on the Face. The climb ended in the worst accident in the history of the Eiger. In two days they had reached the Death Bivouac but then started to retreat, probably because of an injury to Angerer. During the descent the Face was again hit by a storm. Hinterstoisser had opened up the Face with an exceedingly difficult 150-foot traverse below the First Icefield, but when they attempted to reverse the traverse they found the rock impossibly iced up. They attempted to abseil[1] down and one of them fell. He swept another with him, and a third was strangled by the rope. Toni Kurz survived the fall and spent an agonising night in the open. He died of exhaustion the next day, after he had roped down to within ten feet of a rescue party of guides.

Colonel Strutt wrote about what he called 'this insane deed', saying that 'modern German methods of what is misnamed "mountaineering" in that country are, but too often, thoroughly misused, and in every way destructive to the first principles of that pastime as known to every beginner throughout the remainder of Europe.' He agreed with the words quoted in the *Alpine Journal* of one of the Alpine Club's Swiss members, Dr Hug of Zürich: 'The forcing of the Eigerwand [the North Face] is principally a matter of luck – at least 90% of the latter is required. Extreme forms of technical development, a fanatical disregard of death, staying power and bodily toughness are in this case details of mere secondary importance. The incalculable elements of fate, chance, etc. are so overwhelmingly important that this face climb belongs far more to a degenerate form of the Children's Crusade of the Middle Ages.' In his farewell address as retiring President of the Alpine Club in 1938 Colonel Strutt said: 'The Eigerwand continues to be an obsession for the mentally deranged of almost every nation. He who first succeeds may rest assured that he has accomplished the most imbecile variant since mountaineering first began.'

The clash was between generations. The critics of the attempts were conservatives, resisting innovation and change, failing to understand the new mood of climbing. They saw a piton as something that defiled the rock it was banged into; 'any man who put a piton in English rock would shoot a fox' was representative of the classical British attitude. The new climbers were

---

1 Abseil – a method of descent by which the climber slides down a rope fixed at the top. He controls his descent by passing the rope round his body or through a friction device.

'scramblers', 'desperadoes', 'acrobats'. There was also a political tinge to the criticism: the German climbers were accused of attempting the North Face for the glory of the Fatherland.

Old men were criticising the young for trying to reach places they themselves had never dreamt of going to. They ignored the fundamental aspect of climbing: that it is each man's personal choice; that the integrity of a climber's methods are a matter for him alone.

In 1938 the North Face was climbed. Two Germans, Andreas Heckmair and Ludwig Vorg, and two Austrians, Fritz Kasparek and Heinrich Harrer, left Alpiglen in July as two separate ropes, and teamed up when they met on the Face. By the end of the second day they had reached a point near the top of the Ramp, the difficult gangway leading from the top of the Third Icefield to a point level with and to the left of the Spider. The next day they reached the Spider – and then the usual storm came up. The first men ever to reach the Spider quickly discovered that in storms it becomes one long avalanche chute. Several times they were almost hurled from their stances into the void. They bivouacked a third time in the Spider and the next day fought their way up the Exit Cracks and the Summit Icefield.

It was a stupendous achievement, for which the four men had needed to draw on their last reserves of mental and physical energy. They had climbed a face on which eight men had died; they had solved the immense problems of finding a route in that vast upper bowl in a savage storm. They were rewarded for it by fresh outbursts of criticism, even from inside Swiss mountaineering circles. They too were accused of being reckless, fame-seeking, fanatical. The critics still maintained that the Lauper route was the only true route on the Face; the new editor of the *Alpine Journal*, H.E.G. Tyndale, wrote that 'the Eigerwand may be said to possess little or no "mountaineering" value' – even though the new route made a classical attack on the Face, taking advantage of its weaknesses, following the line of least resistance.

The main objection to the route was still that there were too many objective dangers – hazards such as stonefalls and avalanches beyond a climber's control. But on the Lauper route – called by H. E. G. Tyndale 'the true route up the Eiger's North Face' – the objective dangers were even greater, for the sun strikes the North-east Face sooner in the day than the North Face proper, causing the rockfalls to start that much earlier. Two Austrians on the Lauper route in the summer of 1937 found 'avalanches, showers of stones, rushing torrents', with 'every foot of the climb treacherous and slippery'.

The truth is that both routes are dangerous. But if the dangers are beyond a climber's control, he must avoid them. He can avoid stonefalls by studying where and when they occur, and by staying away from the exposed areas at the dangerous times. The North Face of the Eiger was a problem that could be solved by the rigorous application of a climber's skills. It was also a problem that could not be resisted. Climbing is essentially a personal challenge and the new generation of climbers naturally ignored the criticism of their elders. In the years after the war some of the best climbers in Europe climbed the North Face: Buhl (Austrian), Lachenal, Terray and Rebuffat (French). Then came the young Swiss climbers, professional guides also of a new generation: from the Schluneggers in 1947 through to Hilti von Allmen, Ueli Hürlimann, Martin Epp, Paul Etter and Michel Darbellay – who made the first solo ascent – in the 1960s. In 1961 four Germans – again from Munich – made the first winter ascent: Toni Kinshofer, Anderl Mannhardt, Toni Hiebeler and Walter Almberger. The new British climbers were not far behind: Chris Bonington and Ian Clough in 1962, the Rhodesian Rustie Baillie and the Scotsman Dougal Haston in 1963. In making his climb Dougal Haston says he felt at one with the four Germans of 1938 and against their critics; to him they were the fathers of that new generation of climbers of which he was a part.

Another pioneer was Emilio Comici, who in 1935 made the first ascent of the Cima Grande, a sheer limestone wall in the Dolomites. He was two decades ahead of his time in his route-finding concepts: 'Let a drop of water fall directly from the summit and that is the line I want to follow.' By the 1950s climbers were searching for the less prominent routes, tackling them in winter as well as in summer. An increase in climbers' aggressiveness went together with an advance in piton techniques. 1958 was the year of the first great direct, following Comici's edict, and on Comici's own wall, the Cima Grande. Lothar Brandler, Diether Hasse, Jörg Lehne and Siegfried Löw were four young Germans, all of whom had come from Saxony to live – and climb – in the West. They pushed a superb line through the unknown overhangs in the centre of the face. In conception and technique, the route was a significant breakthrough. Direct routes on a number of other Alpine faces followed.

The route taken by every party on the North Face of the Eiger meandered up the line of least resistance. From the foot of the Second Icefield to the top of the Ramp, the route goes almost from one side of the Face to the other, in a gigantic diagonal traverse. Then there is a horizontal traverse back to the Spider in the centre of the Face and a further diagonal line out left to the summit ridge. The Face is 6,000 feet high but the route means 10,000 feet of climbing. The usual reaction of men who climbed the Face was that they never wanted to do so again – the great French pair Terray and Lachenal, who made the second ascent in 1947, said this. But in the 1960s several of the climbers who came off the Face did not share this feeling. In August 1962 John Harlin, a Californian serving in the USAF in Germany, climbed the North Face, the first American to do so. In the spring of 1963 he confided to one of his USAF climbing friends, a dentist called Cleve McCarty, that his ambition was to return to the Face and climb it by a direct route. Dougal Haston also studied the Face carefully during his ascent in 1963 to see if a direct route was possible – and he too came down convinced that it was.

The first two men ever to attempt the Face, Sedlmayer and Mehringer, had followed a line to the top of the Flatiron that was more direct than that used by their successors, though both involved the long diagonal traverse of the Second Icefield. It was their line that the early direct aspirants followed. The first to try were the Poles Crestaw Momatiuk and Jan Mostowsky. Mostowsky had climbed the normal route in 1961. The pair were defeated by a storm before they really got to grips with the problem, being forced to turn back before they reached the steep wall below the First Icefield. In July 1963 three Dolomite guides, Lorenzo Lorenzi, Bruno Menardi and Albino Michielli, members of the group known as the Cortina Squirrels, made an attempt. They followed a line to the left of the Sedlmayer–Mehringer line but were turned back at some fierce overhangs below the First Icefield.

That same summer the Italians Ignazio Piussi and Roberto Sorgato, who the previous winter had made the first winter ascent of the direct route on the north face of the Civetta in the Dolomites, were turned back by bad weather on two separate occasions. On neither did they make much progress. John Harlin also returned to the Face for the first time. He camped at Alpiglen but the weather was never good enough even for a reconnaissance climb.

In January 1964 came the most serious attempt yet, made by a well-qualified team based on Munich – Peter Siegert, Reiner Kauschke, Werner Bittner and Gert Uhner, all Saxons. The first three had made the first winter direct ascent of the north face of the Cima Grande, a 'superdirettissima' that took seventeen days. Probably overanxious to start, they left Kleine Scheidegg for the Face when it was still deep in powder snow. In three days, one of which they spent bivouacked during a storm, they struggled up to the foot of the steep cliff below the First Icefield. More bad weather was forecast, so they climbed in through a window in the Jungfrau railway tunnel, and returned to Kleine Scheidegg by train.

The next month John Harlin was back – not for an attempt on the direct, but to try to make the second winter ascent. But he had to turn back at the Hinterstoisser traverse below the First Icefield because his climbing partner had become ill. At Scheidegg he found that the Italians Piussi and Sorgato, with their compatriots Marcello Bonafede and Natalino Menegus, were preparing for the direct, and he joined up with them. In three days they had reached the First Icefield but turned back when they heard by radio that bad weather was approaching.

The following June John Harlin was back again with Sorgato and Piussi and the two French climbers, René Desmaison and André Bertrand. This was the best attempt so far: carrying heavy rucksacks, they spent four nights bivouacked on the Face and reached the top of the Second Icefield, precisely following the Sedlmayer–Mehringer line. But once again bad weather forced them down.

John Harlin came back to the Eiger for the fourth time in the winter of 1964. This time he had with him Dougal Haston, who had climbed the normal route in the summer of 1963. Their attempt was not too serious, being more of a reconnaissance than anything else. They went out of a tunnel window on the Jungfrau railway and spent the first day climbing from there to the foot of the great cliff below the First Icefield which extended from one side of the Face to the other, and which they now knew as the First Band. The next day they tackled the cliff, climbing several pitches.[1] The standard of difficulty was grade VI, the hardest of all. On the third day they traversed below the First Band to the Eigerwand station and examined the climbing problems there. They looked extreme, and the climbers came off the Face a little subdued. The rock had been covered with powder snow; the icefields were hard ice that would need steps in them all the way. 'It would take three weeks,' they told each other, half in jest, half in despair.

John had hoped to try the direct late the next summer with the British climber Chris Bonington. But the Face never came into condition. When autumn came John began to lay plans for another attempt that winter. News filtered through that a German climber, Peter Haag, was in secret training in the Black Forest with a team who later invited John to join them. Haag planned to use rope-ladders so that his support team could follow up easily, it was reported. The Italians Piussi and Sorgato were known still to be keen; so, too, was the Frenchman René Desmaison. 'People are thinking about it all over Europe,' observed the Swiss guide Hilti von Allmen in November 1965. The Eiger direct had become known as the last great problem in the Alps. Would that winter see it climbed?

---

1 Pitches – the natural sections of a climb, limited either by the length of the climbing rope – normally between 120 and 150 feet – or by the availability of good belay stances.

# Chapter II

John Harlin was born in Kansas City in 1935. His father worked for Transworld Airlines and travelled a great deal. John spent several long periods in Ireland and France. For a time in France the family had a home at Versailles with eleven acres of ground, and this helped develop in him a love of the wild. He also had an early flair for excitement: one of Mrs Harlin's neighbours complained that John was taking other children for walks across the rooftops of Paris. The last high school he attended was at Sequoia in California. He went from there to Stanford University, where he majored in fine arts and dress design. He spent part of one summer working for Balmain in Paris.

When he was a boy his father had taken him on hunting and fishing trips. He enjoyed these, but when he was eighteen he decided that the animals he was killing had as much right to live as he had. He consciously searched for another sport offering the same involvement with nature and discovered climbing. He was introduced into Stanford Climbing Club by Jon Lindbergh, son of the aviator. Two years later, in 1954, he made his first attempt on the North Face of the Eiger by the normal route, but without getting very far.

He married his wife Marilyn, whom he had met in the climbing club, the next year – just after he had been on the north face of the Matterhorn, at the age of twenty.

In 1957 he received a commission in the United States Air Force. He chose to stay in five years because it was the only way he could become a pilot, and in flying he found something of the exhilaration of climbing. 'The aircraft was in my hands and the sky the dimension of my youth,' he wrote in an account of one of his climbs. 'Whether flying or mountain climbing, the sky had become more than a playground.'

Because he came top of his training class in the Air Force, he could choose what assignment he was sent on. He went to Germany so that he could climb in the Alps. He would drive from Hahn air base on a Friday night to Chamonix or the Dolomites, bivouac out on Saturday night and drive back to base on Sunday night.

In August 1962 he climbed the Eiger by the normal route. He made the attempt, he wrote, 'because it was one of the toughest mountaineering problems in the world'. He spent two days fighting his way up from the Spider in a bad storm, saving the lives of two Swiss climbers in severe difficulties. This was the first American ascent, and was made before any British climber was successful.

In June 1963 he left active service in the Air Force and the same year became Director of Sports at the American School in Leysin in Switzerland. A year later he left the American School to start with four other climbers the International School of Modern Mountaineering in Leysin. In 1965 the partnership was joined by the English climber Bev Clark, and that year the first pupils came to the school. The school had an eclectic approach, teaching the best of each country's climbing methods.

By 1966 John had put up three important new routes in Europe. In 1963, with the Americans Tom Frost, Stuart Fulton and Gary Hemming, he climbed the south face of the Fou, one of the last remaining problems in the Chamonix Aiguilles. The same year, with Tom Frost, he climbed the Hidden Pillar of Frêney, a new route on the western Frêney face of Mont Blanc. He also made the second winter ascent of the north face of the Mönch in 1964: he and the Swiss guide Martin Epp took ten hours against the first party's four days. In 1965, with the American Royal Robbins, he put up a new direct route on the south-west face of the Dru, one of the most beautiful of the Chamonix Aiguilles. The new route, following a big line of cracks up the face, was a significant breakthrough in alpine climbing standards.

John was a superb athlete, with a passion to excel. He was in the all-American Services football team. He was junior wrestling champion of California. He came twenty-fifth in the world *Langlauf* championships six months after starting to ski. At the age of thirty he could still run 100 yards in 9.7 seconds: Dougal Haston was out in the snow with him once and threw a snowball at him and started to run away. 'He just came at me, picked me up, and threw me down a bank,' said Dougal. John was also in the USAF formation-flying team.

He had a sophisticated, sensual approach to the experience of climbing. He searched for the direct lines, calling them 'the aesthetic lines of attack'. He wrote of the normal route on the south face of the Fou, following a diagonal crack rising from right to left, that it 'only tastes the face and does not devour or savour it'. He delighted in the physical act of climbing: of one climb he wrote: 'In placing those pitons and in stretching for the infrequent holds on that great smooth wall, life effervesced within me.' A major reason why he climbed was that on the mountain he was his own master, a free agent making decisions about his own situation and acting on them. Of a grim moment on his 1962 Eiger climb he wrote: 'I felt completely beaten, a man without an acceptable alternative.' The best moments of climbing were when he could achieve a perfect balance between his physical and mental capabilities; and the moments of complete trust and understanding between himself and his climbing partners.

He saw climbing as a means to internationalism, because of the opportunities it gave people from different countries to work together in harmony. 'Because of the connotations of fellowship, non-competitiveness, mutual understanding and enjoyment, climbing can be a vehicle in the sustenance of peace.'

Apart from these reasons, climbing was an experience fully valued for itself. He used his typically American facility for self-analysis to explore his reactions to what was happening. The most striking example of this was during his 1962 Eiger climb, when he saw the storm clouds approaching. He estimated the storm would hit the face in four hours. His partner started to pull their bivouac tent over them. But John did not use it. He wrote afterwards: 'I felt strongly that if this was going to be the beginning of the end I wanted to absorb all of the visual stimuli I could aesthetically enjoy.'

He had a serious exterior, which made people imagine at first that he had no sense of humour. When he first met people he would test them, exploring their loyalties and their own sense of seriousness. Once he had accepted them, his friendship, consideration and generosity were unlimited. But beneath his seriousness, his ability to articulate about himself and his motives, lay a certain restlessness. He was always looking beyond the here and now, dreaming, laying plans. His ambitiousness went together with an all-embracing optimism that sometimes annoyed climbers from the tradition of British realism, such as Don Whillans.

For the Eiger North Face direct he needed many of these qualities: drive, ambition, an ability to plan, optimism. He was going to have to draw on his ten years' knowledge of the Alps, to apply what he had learnt about mountains and their moods, in the most deadly test of his proficiency as a mountaineer. In November 1965 he said: 'A climb like that has to be the culmination of one's climbing experience.'

John first met Layton Kor in the spring of 1964, at a meeting of the American Alpine Club in Boston at which John was the annual speaker. He talked on 'The Problem of the Eiger Direct and the Mood of Alpine Climbing'. 'He explained he'd been on the Face a couple of times without getting anywhere,' said Layton. 'He'd had bad weather and the wrong companions.' By that time Layton himself was known as one of America's best rock climbers. He had been climbing since 1954, and was a bricklayer by trade. He would earn enough in four or five months of the year to climb for the rest.

From the start, compared with British climbers, he'd got it made. Londoners have to drive 250 miles to Wales for any real climbing. A short drive from his home in Boulder, Colorado, were the towering sandstone cliffs of Eldorado Canyon, offering practice routes of up to 700 feet. One day when he was sixteen he saw a television film about climbing. The next day he went out with a geological axe to cut steps in the rock – 'I thought that was how it was done.' Very soon he was leading new routes.

Layton grew to be six feet four inches tall, and he made full use of his phenomenal reach. People following him up a route frequently had to devise a completely different way of doing the climb. His bridging would often be impossible for ordinary men; he could reach holds above him that were out of the question for other climbers. On artificial routes he would place pitons so far apart that the second would be in severe difficulties when it came to taking them out.

His chief drive to climb appeared to be an unresting nervous energy – the same restlessness that pushed him from one job and one place to another. On the ground he was never really happy until he could start climbing again.

He put up an immense number of new routes on the virgin mountains and faces of the United States, from Colorado to Alaska, including the Western Buttress on El Capitan, the monstrous 3,000-foot granite face in Yosemite National Park. One route he did not climb was the ugly, incredibly difficult North America Wall, first climbed in 1964. 'That's not a route you just go and climb. It takes you months to work up to it,' he explained.

He liked his climbing to be enjoyable: he was not in the tradition of the seriously minded, philosophising American climber. He complained that one climber had said that a sunrise creeping up the face towards a bivouac site had been 'better than Mozart'. 'Better than Mozart – can you imagine it? Everyone afterwards said it had been better than Fats Domino.' He liked partners who could laugh on a climb, even in difficult situations. 'It's no good when they go white and start shaking and lose a grip of themselves.' He himself had been in and fought his way through a number of hair-raising situations. In 1962, he and a partner, Jim Marts, made the first ascent of an 1,800-foot pillar in Black Canyon in western Colorado. He had told Marts that it never rained there – but when they were half-way up an immense thunderstorm broke. Layton was soaked, with rainwater filling his boots, and the top pitches turned out to be immensely loose and thin. Layton placed some pitons for aid but they were shaken out of their cracks and slid down the rope to accumulate around Marts' waist. By now it was pitch dark and Layton was climbing with a flashlight in his mouth – only for the batteries to burn out before he reached the top. Despite the mistakes, it was an example of Layton's inspired climbing.

He had lost seven close friends in the ten years he had been climbing, though never while he was actually climbing with them. But he was never hardened to death.

After the American Alpine Club meeting, the next contact between John and Layton was when John sent a Christmas card in 1964. Layton decided he couldn't very well send one back as it was already after Christmas when the card arrived. Next spring, when he was thinking of coming to Europe to climb,

Layton wrote to John and asked him about the European climbing scene, but John didn't reply – 'I was pissed off with him not replying to *my* letter,' John explained later. 'I never got any *letter*,' Layton protested. Anyway, Layton then wrote to Royal Robbins, another Yosemite expert who was teaching skiing at the Leysin American school. Layton worked in Colorado for three months in the summer and then came to Europe by boat in October. He went straight to Leysin because Royal Robbins and John were the only two Americans he knew in Europe. To his delight, he found the British climbers Don Whillans and Mick Burke working there too. 'That was a pretty good selection of climbers.' At Leysin Layton did six new routes, principally on and around the Sphinx, a 500-foot limestone face. He climbed with Don Whillans, Royal Robbins and Yvon Chouinard, another Yosemite man – Chouinard makes climbing equipment and he was in Europe on a business trip.

One of the routes Layton had in mind to do in Europe was the Eiger direct, but in summer. He knew John himself was very interested in the direct. When he arrived at Leysin he found that John was talking hard about doing it that winter. Then one day late in November John met Layton and said he would like him to come on the climb. 'I'd like you to think about it carefully and decide in a week,' John said. 'Once you come in I want you to commit yourself completely.' Layton said he was interested right away. From that moment he was one of the team.

John and Dougal had known each other since the summer of 1963, when they had been introduced in the Bar National, hang-out of British climbers in Chamonix. Dougal was one of Britain's best young climbers. He came from Currie, near Edinburgh, and his father was a baker. From the age of twelve he used to go walking on the Pentlands, the nearest hills to Edinburgh, either alone or with friends such as James Moriarty – known as Big Elly – who were to become future climbing companions. The walking began to involve scrambling and then a little climbing. At the same time Dougal had a passion for climbing the brickwork of railway bridges.

When they were sixteen Dougal and Elly joined the Junior Mountaineering Club of Scotland. One of the best Scottish climbers of the time was Jimmy Marshall, whose younger brother they knew well. One day they were on a JMCS meet when Jimmy Marshall saw them climbing. He told them to tie on to his rope. 'It was a kind of a game,' recalls Big Elly. 'He kept taking us up harder and harder things but we followed them all.' After that Dougal went climbing with Jimmy Marshall quite often, and it was Jimmy who introduced Dougal to his first major Scottish routes.

Soon afterwards, Dougal began to go to the Alps for summer seasons, either with Elly or with Robin Smith, one of his closest climbing companions until he and Wilfred Noyce died in a fall in the Pamirs. 'We were so confident then,' said Dougal. 'I went to the Dolomites when I was eighteen and we went straight on to pitches of six superior. We just didn't understand big mountains.'

'Confident' was right. On one of his first visits he and Elly made an early ascent of the Gabriel–Lavanos route on the Cima Su Alto in the Dolomites, then considered one of the hardest free routes in the Alps. 'We were travelling light,' says Dougal. 'We just had to get to the top in a day.' They wore jeans, sweaters and anoraks. They had no food and no bivouac gear. They reached the top in a thunderstorm just as it was getting dark. They didn't know the way down and they had nothing with which to protect themselves from the storm, so they just lay down on the summit in the pouring rain and waited for morning.

When morning came they still didn't know the way down. They found some abseil pegs at the top of a couloir, so started roping down it, huge free 150-foot abseils. On the third or fourth abseil the rope stuck. They couldn't hope to climb back up to free it as it ran straight up through a waterfall. Dougal climbed back up as far as he could and cut it, bringing down a 40-foot length. They carried on abseiling on that. Near the bottom they came to a series of overhangs. They tried a number of places, but nowhere did the rope appear to reach anywhere near the ground. Eventually they got fed up, so Dougal none the less threw the rope over and set off down it, prepared to jump the last part of the way. Fortunately for him and history, the rope was short by only ten feet.

In 1959 he and Robin Smith went on to the north face of the Matterhorn, again wearing jeans and Marks and Spencer sweaters. They decided their lack of equipment was no problem as they could undoubtedly reach the summit in a day, but bad weather forced them back after they had covered the first 1,200 feet in an hour. They were seen coming back down by Toni Hiebeler, a member of the team that made the first winter ascent of the Eiger and editor of the German climbing magazine *Alpinismus*. Hiebeler later published a whole issue about British climbing: and in a rather patronising article described how he had seen two British climbers in jeans and sweaters on the north face of the Matterhorn, using this to substantiate his inference that British climbers as a whole were thoughtless and ill-equipped.

At the end of the 1959 season Dougal and Robin Smith went to the Eiger. Dougal's boots had long gaps between the seams and uppers, and neither of them had anything sophisticated like gaiters. For food they took with them a few pieces of bread and some sugar. Fortunately bad weather drove them back. 'We had this primitive urge for big routes,' Dougal explained.

In Scotland Dougal was beginning to put up new routes, particularly in winter, and particularly on Ben Nevis and in Glencoe. He was one of several Scottish climbers pushing ice-climbing standards further and further ahead, treating ice as the tigers of the 1950s treated rock. Long run-outs, tiny holds, poor protection and extremely steep routes became normal. Dougal was soon climbing an average of twenty-five new routes a year. In the summers he was climbing his way through most of the major routes in the Alps.

In 1962 he went on to the Eiger again, with a Scottish friend, Andy Wightman. The weather was not good but they pressed on to the Third Icefield. To their dismay, they saw ahead of them six Italian climbers strung out along the whole length of the Ramp, and moving very slowly. There was now no chance of a quick finish, so they bivouacked on the Flatiron and started back down the next day. Conditions by now were very bad: the Second Icefield was running with water. They climbed down the Difficult Crack in a cloudburst, and then unroped so that they could get down quickly. Dougal negotiated an overhang, but when Andy tried to follow he fell off from sheer tiredness. He fell 20 feet and stopped right on the edge of a 1,500-foot drop.

Dougal went down to him and found that his ankle was broken. Fortunately two Italian climbers were bivouacked nearby and they had seen all this happen. They climbed up to the Stollenloch, one of the Jungfraubahn tunnel windows, fixed a rope to it, and dropped it down the 150 feet to Dougal and Andy. Dougal tied on to it and heaved Andy on his shoulders. With the two Italians pulling them in, Andy grabbed at what handholds he could while Dougal used his feet. They reached the tunnel and Dougal and the two Italians then had to carry Andy up the tunnel to the Eigerwand station. This was after Dougal had spent two days on the Face, one of them retreating in storm. 'I was so exhausted I just came through the other side,' he says.

Nothing daunted, Dougal went back to the Eiger the next year, and with the Rhodesian climber Rustie Baillie made the second British ascent, in a fast time. At the time he was a student of philosophy at Edinburgh University, but shortly afterwards he effectively renounced his course and started a climbing school in Glencoe in partnership with Bev Clark, John Harlin's former partner at Leysin.

The youthful confidence with which Dougal first went to the Alps matured into a hardened, thorough approach, leaving nothing to chance. Deeply reflective about climbing, he realised that it alone brought him more than momentary satisfaction in life. Together with his calm, quiet appearance, went a stubbornness with which he tackled the problems of life and of climbing. His goals weren't vague: he knew exactly what they were and how he could achieve them.

Dougal's first climb with John was in 1964 when they attempted a new route on the Shroud, an ice climb in the Chamonix range. That winter they went on to the Eiger for a direct reconnaissance together. In September 1965 John first asked Dougal about an attempt the following winter. Dougal said that he was interested. John came to England that Christmas and called Dougal from Bev Clark's mews house near Marble Arch. He asked Dougal if he'd like to join the team, and Dougal agreed.

On 14 January John phoned Dougal from Switzerland and asked: 'Are you prepared to come to Switzerland at short notice?' Dougal said he was and promptly went off climbing in Scotland with Bev.

Two weeks later they came down from spending three days on Ben Nevis and found a note tucked under the windscreen of Bev's Mini Cooper S. It was from John. He had rung Bev's wife in London; she had rung Dougal's girlfriend in Edinburgh; she had rung Graham Tiso, the owner of an Edinburgh climbing equipment shop and a climbing friend of Dougal's; he had rung Hamish McInnes, a climber who lived in Glencoe; and he had rung a friend in Fort William who had fixed the message on to the car. It said: 'Please ring at once. John.' Bev rang Switzerland and found that John wanted Dougal out there straight away. Dougal phoned a message through to say that he was leaving and caught a plane from Edinburgh the next day, 1 February. He was on his way.

The next morning Dougal arrived at Leysin by the rack railway that climbs up from the Rhône Valley. 'I stood on the platform at the rear of a crowd of people with a huge rucksack on my back. John reached through the crowd, grabbed my hand, and pulled me through. Within five minutes we were discussing the route.'

There was plenty to talk about. The team still weren't sure which route they would follow. There were two possibilities. One was to follow the route taken by Sedlmayer and Mehringer to the point where they had died, known ever since as the Death Bivouac, and then strike directly up to the summit. All previous attempts had followed this line. The other possibility was a virgin line starting about a quarter of a mile to the left, directly below the windows of the Eigerwand station. It was a route that climbers could hardly help noticing – Toni Hiebeler had considered it for his winter ascent in 1961, for example. It was purer than the Sedlmayer–Mehringer route, following a very definite line on the Face. The climbing would be interesting all the way from the foot of the Face to the summit, whereas the Sedlmayer–Mehringer route covered known ground up to the Death Bivouac, and used the normal route for the whole of the Second Icefield. But the overriding advantage of the new line was that it was more direct.

The three – John, Layton and Dougal – met in John's chalet in Leysin to talk it over. Pictures of the Face littered the floor; as a backdrop they had Mont Blanc and the Chamonix Aiguilles rising from the other side of the Rhône Valley. But once they thought about the problem, they realised how little choice there really was. The new left-hand route, as well as being a far more aesthetic line, was much more a true direct. They felt compelled to go for it. The natural line up the greatest face in the Alps was an irresistible challenge.

So within a day they had decided on the route. This done, the climbing problems facing them were immense, of a scale and difficulty never before tackled in the Alps. Any one of these problems could end the attempt. The first was the 300-foot cliff above the Eigerwand station, known as the First Band. The previous winter, when they were coming off their direct attempt, John and Dougal made the traverse below the First Band to have a close look at a possible route for an attempt the following year. They stopped at what appeared to be its narrowest section, just to the right of the Eigerwand station. All they could see, rising sheer above them, was a blank wall with a few thin cracks in it. 'Let's look round the corner for a better line,' said John. The nearest corner was 1,000 feet further on, so the two came down instead.

Five hundred feet above the First Band came the route's next problem – a steep cliff cut by vertical ice gullies which they called, with due logic, the Second Band. This, too, was an unknown factor. It looked as though a highly skilled ice-climber could find a way up the gullies – providing the ice in them was continuous. Where ice occurs in broken stretches, the sections just below rock are always rotten and it is extremely difficult to climb out of them.

Above the Second Band the team thought they would be able to find a gully system taking them to the left of the Flatiron, the 800-foot buttress at the left-hand end of the Second Icefield. But they held in mind the possibility of traversing right at the foot of the Flatiron and climbing straight up the left-hand end of the Second Icefield.

From the top of the Flatiron they thought they would drop down on to the Third Icefield and climb one pitch on the Ramp, the steep leftward-slanting ledge used on the normal route. But from there they would strike right again, into a system of ice gullies that John had christened the White Pony, the shape they seemed to have when seen from the air. From there some extremely hard rock climbing in a chimney system would lead to the top of a pillar 300 feet below the Spider. A traverse to the right would take them to a ramp leading into the Spider – two members of the team would tackle this, leaving their sacks on the top of the pillar. When they got into the Spider they would drop a rope straight down to the top of the pillar to bring their sacks and the third man up.

From the Spider they would climb to what John called a 'lacework of icebands' to the Fly, a second, smaller icefield that seems from Kleine Scheidegg to be caught in the Spider's gigantic web. Ice gullies appeared to lead from the Fly to the top of another pillar. From there a system of difficult cracks and chimneys trended left to the summit ridge. They would come out about 250 feet below the summit, to its right, and walk up the easy-angled ridge to the corniced peak.

This was the theory. But question marks remained. How much of a barrier was the smooth, vertical First Band? How good was the ice in the gullies penetrating the Second Band? Would the route go above the Fly? John decided an aerial reconnaissance could provide the answers. He rang up Hermann

Geiger, the most experienced pilot flying in the Alps, who runs a company, Glacier-Pilots, based at Sion airport in the Rhône Valley. Could he take them to have a close look at the Face? Yes, he could: he arrived at Leysin in a six-seater helicopter on 2 February.

The journey took twenty minutes. It was Layton's first view of the Face. 'I'm not usually impressed by a face until I get on it. But I was pretty impressed this time. It was the biggest face I'd seen – twice as big as El Cap' – the 3,000-foot wall in Yosemite with some of the most impressive and frightening climbing in the United States.

Layton, as the rock expert, examined what was to be one of his particular problems, the First Band. Dougal – the ice man – tried to work out exactly what climbing the Second Band would entail. He also thought he could see a line rising almost perfectly direct from the Fly to the summit, to the left of the one chosen by John. In retrospect this turned out to be the most valuable piece of information he acquired.

John took still and movie photographs of the route during the flight. The Face was so immense that they required ten separate runs at different levels to see all they wanted to. Sitting in the tiny helicopter that buzzed past the Face like some insignificant insect, Dougal became very much aware of the immensity of the problems facing them. But they were encouraged by what they saw. The route was hard, there was no doubt about that: it was probably harder than anything previously attempted in the Alps. But it would definitely go.[1]

These, then, were the pure climbing problems of the attempt. On top of these were the logistics of the climb: the vast organisational task of keeping three men alive and healthy for however long the climb should take; of getting them and all the equipment they needed from point A, the foot of the Face, to point B, the summit. The team planned to make an Alpine-style ascent of the Face; that is, they would climb the Face in one continuous push, carrying all their equipment with them as they went. They would spend the nights in the open, bivouacking on ledges. The sole reason why they were going on the route in winter was that, because of the cold, the danger of stonefalls was immensely cut down. The loose rubble that pours off the Face in summer would be simply frozen in place. John reasoned that it was usual to have at least two ten-day spells of good weather every winter. It was therefore just a question of waiting until one of these periods was forecast before leaving Kleine Scheidegg and blasting for the top.

The first basic problem of the logistics of the assault was the clothes the climbers would wear. They would have to withstand ten days of extremely cold weather. They needed to be sufficiently well protected to survive if they were

---

1 Go – prove climbable.

caught in a storm. 'If a storm comes and we're below the Spider we go down; if we're above it we go up,' John said. Either way could involve one or two days' climbing. Climbers had died on the Face in *summer* storms, and John himself had spent two days fighting for his life in one in 1962, held up by a slower party who had got into difficulties.

The three men in the team wore boots that John himself had designed. He had felt the need for a double boot that was light enough not to hamper difficult rock climbing. Working with Le Phoque, a small specialist firm of boot-makers with a factory at Izeaux (Isère) in France, he produced a prototype that was essentially an ordinary single boot with a felt inner. Dougal tried it out when he and John had attempted a new route on the Shroud. Conditions for testing the boot were ideal, for the pair were caught in a shattering storm. They had a bad bivouac and spent the whole of the next day retreating in the blizzard. They were badly frightened when a lightning-bolt clattered into the snow just ten yards from where they were climbing, during a traverse off the Shroud to the Walker. But when they reached Chamonix Dougal's feet were intact.

John modified the boots, designing a proper outer boot and reinforcing the felt inner with suede. Dougal wore these for an attempt on the first winter ascent of the Pillar of Frêney, the route on which four men died in a storm in the summer of 1963. Because reaching the foot of the Pillar is a major climb in itself, John and Dougal climbed to the summit of Mont Blanc by the normal route, intending to abseil down the Pillar and climb back up again. But they were hit by a storm on the top of Mont Blanc and again had to retreat in appalling conditions. John was not wearing his own boots and his feet were on the verge of frostbite; Dougal's were again unharmed.

For the direct attempt, the team added a second inner layer by cutting up Marilyn Harlin's hand-me-down fur coat. 'It was probably only a rabbit one,' Dougal explained. 'Anyway, it gave us that vital extra layer of insulation.'

They wore only one pair of socks each. More than one restricts circulation and makes boots more difficult to climb in.

Over their socks they wore gaiters. These were specially designed for them by the French equipment firm of Millet. Gaiters that are pulled on over the feet would be useless in the bivouac conditions they were going to encounter. Millet produced three pairs that zipped up instead, and with the zip conveniently at the side instead of awkwardly at the back.

To go over their boots and gaiters they had Millet overboots: giant sock-shaped coverings made of canvas and plastic that are normally used for snow climbing. But they cut the bottoms out so that they could climb on rock as well and kept them in place by strapping their crampons over them.

Layton and Dougal both wore all-wool climbing breeches, ending just below their knees, from Snell Sport in Chamonix. John wore ski-trousers, for the devious reason that he liked to carry as many spare socks as possible: wearing ski-trousers meant that he could wear short socks instead of long ones and therefore carry more spare pairs with him. All three wore all-wool long johns underneath their trousers, and John wore a silk pair as well. They chose wool for as many clothes as possible because, unlike cotton or down, it retains some of its warmth when it is wet.

On top of everything they wore overtrousers made of polyurethene and nylon. They started off with two pairs each, but by the time the climb was over they had used up sixteen pairs among them. Putting overtrousers on while wearing crampons turned out to be a highly skilled operation which the exigencies of the moment sometimes prevented them from carrying out with the care it required.

The team kept to wool also for the upper half of their bodies: they each had a cashmere wool undershirt, a woollen shirt, a light Shetland wool sweater, and a heavy sweater on top of that. They each had a down jacket and a polyurethene parka as well. An important design point was that the parkas zipped up the front, unlike cagoules, which have to be pulled on over the head. Because cagoules cannot be opened down the front they cause sweating. If it is cold, the sweat then freezes and the inside of the cagoule ices up. But they did carry cagoules in reserve, as it is important to wear two waterproof layers in storm conditions.

Each man had three pairs of gloves: silk inners, which they would wear for difficult rock climbing if they were going to wear gloves at all; woollen mitts, which they would put on for mixed climbing; and waterproof outer mitts, making three layers in all, for snow work.

Finally, each man had a crash helmet – essential even in winter when, although stonefalls are far fewer than in summer, they are still a considerable danger.

This completed the list of clothing they reckoned they would need. The next problem was the equipment they should take. In every case they looked for the best that was available, but always considering the essential question of weight.

Ropes were obviously of vital importance. For a long time John and Dougal had been looking for a rope that didn't freeze up. Finally they found one, made by the Swiss firm of Mammoth. John asked the firm to supply him with three 100-metre lengths of 7-millimetre perlon for sack-hauling and four 50-metre lengths of 11-millimetre perlon for climbing. The firm's director, Herr H. Weber, generously gave them to the team.

Layton and Dougal were given the task of deciding what rock- and ice-climbing aids would be needed. The most advanced rock hardware is produced in the USA and Layton knew exactly what was the latest available. Some of it had to be ordered directly from the States. He chose some sixty pegs of various shapes and angles, chiefly made of Chromolly, a high-strength steel alloy developed by the American equipment manufacturer Yvon Chouinard. Dougal organised the ice-equipment. He chose three short ice-axes and three Asmu ice-daggers, and one long axe for whoever would be leading across the deep snow on the approach to the Face. Dougal himself had a gully hammer given to him by Hamish McInnes. He ordered twenty Salewa and ten Marwa ice-screws and twenty-four assorted ice-pegs. They made themselves six snow-pickets for anchoring belays in deep snow by cutting down a selection of ski-poles that had been lying around the basement of John's chalet. Finally, they each had a pair of Salewa adjustable crampons.

Then came the bivouac gear. They bought a Whillans tent-sack to drape over themselves as they sat on whatever ledge they found to spend the night on. They each had a Terray down sleeping bag. They had a paraffin Primus stove, with a Camping Gas stove in reserve. Fauve Leuba of Geneva gave them a bivouac watch, complete with altimeter and barometer, which they could keep if they got to the summit. And for the vital Face-to-ground radio link, which would keep them informed of the latest weather reports, they took a pair of short-wave walkie-talkies. To carry all this equipment, they bought themselves three Millet Desmaison rucksacks.

The equipment cost several hundred pounds, presenting an obvious and immediate problem of finance. For their projected summer attempt John and Chris Bonington had secured the backing of the *Weekend Telegraph*, the colour magazine that appears weekly with the London *Daily Telegraph*. After the summer climb proved unfeasible, the financial arrangements were carried over to the winter attempt.

The next logistical problem was how to keep three human beings alive in one of the most hostile environments anywhere in the world. This was a question John had studied closely. His Air Force training meant that he was familiar with the problem and the terms in which it was discussed. He had read abstracts on aviation medicine, and had written a paper himself. His wife was teacher of chemistry and biology at the Leysin American school and he had discussed it with her.

'People get surprised and upset on the mountain when things start going wrong,' he had told Peter Gillman when they first met the previous November. 'Why the hell after three or four bivouacs am I pissing every five minutes and getting weaker?' For brews in bivouacs climbers have to melt down snow, and the water is almost completely distilled. An ionic imbalance between the water the climber drinks and the water in his cells results. 'You just piss it right out of you,' John explained. 'Somehow you have to replace the minerals you are losing.' To do this the team bought stocks of Calcitonic, containing calcium and Vitamin C; mineral and vitamin tablets; a Swiss vitamin drink called Minivit; and rose-hip tea.

They ordered five kilos of *viande sechée des Grisons* – a dried meat with one of the highest protein contents available – and three kilos of bacon. For 'instant energy' they stocked up with chocolate and nuts, and dried fruit completed the list.

But the actual food they were to take on the climb was only half the story. 'There's your physiological conditioning,' said John. 'For example, your body has to learn that it can sacrifice its extremities to keep the rest warm.' Like Hermann Buhl, John carried snowballs around in his bare hands; and he, Dougal and Layton skied around without gloves as a matter of course all winter. 'You have to do this because on the Eiger there are going to be a great many places where you can't wear gloves. And by doing this sort of thing you can increase the size of your spleen, which gives you more red blood cells,' John explained.

When they had finished planning all their equipment they reckoned that each man would have to carry 50 pounds in his rucksack and a further 20 pounds of climbing hardware hung around his body. The total weight was way beyond that normally carried on an alpine climb. The four Germans who made the first winter ascent of the North Face in 1961 carried rucksacks weighing only 25 pounds and a further 20 pounds of climbing equipment each. But there was nothing for it but to grin and literally bear it. Every single piece of equipment was going to be vital in the ten-day battle facing them.

# Chapter III

When Layton, John and Dougal made the helicopter reconnaissance on Wednesday 2 February, the Face was in superb condition: the rock was mostly free of powder snow and the icefields seemed to be covered with snow that was packed hard. They decided to move to Kleine Scheidegg as quickly as possible in order to get on the Face as soon as the next spell of good weather came.

They spent 3 February in a panic, rushing round Leysin buying last-minute supplies and equipment, and then piling all their gear into John's micro-bus. That afternoon they drove to Scheidegg.

They arrived at Lauterbrunnen half an hour before the last train left for Scheidegg. The Jungfrau railway runs from Lauterbrunnen to the west of Scheidegg and Grindelwald to the east. The lines meet at Scheidegg and continue as one to the Jungfrau hotel on the ridge between the Eiger's neighbours, the Mönch and the Jungfrau. John, Dougal and Layton caught the train, and as they came up the valley from Wengernalp they could see the West Flank of the Eiger and then the North Face, half-hidden in cloud.

At Scheidegg they had taken two rooms in the Villa Maria, part of the main Scheidegg hotels but on the wrong side of the railway track. They had the rooms at a cheap rate conceded to them by Fritz von Almen, the owner of the hotels. When they arrived at the station, they found a large parcel containing the perlon ropes given to them by Mammoth Ropeworks: the ropes were coloured bright red and yellow and were beautifully clean and new. They quickly turned the top floor of the Villa Maria into their base camp, spreading equipment across the landing between their two rooms and piling it into every available corner.

As part of their coverage of the climb, the *Weekend Telegraph* had asked Chris Bonington to go as photographer with the team to the foot of the First Band. When the First Band had been climbed he was to come back to Scheidegg and then go up the West Flank and shoot pictures from there. He was also to meet the team on the summit.

Chris was one of Britain's most experienced and accomplished alpinists. He had made the first British ascent of the normal route on the North Face with Ian Clough in 1962; the first ascent of the Central Pillar of Frêney on Mont Blanc with Don Whillans, Ian Clough and a Polish climber; the first ascents of Nuptse and Annapurna II in the Himalaya and of the Central Tower of Paine in the Peruvian Andes. He was one of Britain's handful of professional climbers, faced with the eternal problem of how to climb and earn money at the same time. When he left school Chris had become a professional soldier, going through Sandhurst and taking five years to reach the lordly rank of second lieutenant in a tank regiment. He then decided he had had enough of learning how to kill people and left the army. After some time spent climbing, he married and became a margarine salesman. This lasted for six months before he chucked the job and went on a climbing expedition to the Andes, taking his wife Wendy with him. When he came home he started to make a living in the untidy collection of ways open to climbers: he gave lectures, advised an equipment firm, started writing his autobiography and tried his hand at journalism. He wrote an article for the *Weekend Telegraph* early in 1965 and the assignment to cover the Eiger direct followed, after his own summer attempt did not materialise.

When John arrived at Scheidegg on Friday 4 February, he asked if Chris could join the party at once. If Chris was coming with them for the first two or three days he would need to be there right away to avoid delaying the start. But on 5 February Chris was in North Wales helping the BBC plan a climbing outside-broadcast, and intended to fly to Zürich on 7 February. John was worried in case even this was too late, and he rang up the *Telegraph*. Late that afternoon, Peter Gillman, the *Weekend Telegraph* writer who would be reporting the climb, was given the job of tracking Chris down.

Peter had been editor of *Isis* at Oxford, spent a badly paid year on a London glossy magazine 'for men', and moved to the *Weekend Telegraph* in August 1964. He was a climber himself, and when he heard that the *Telegraph* was backing an attempt on the direct, he suggested that he and the photographer John Cleare did a background story on the Eiger and the new route. They went to Switzerland to do this in November 1965, meeting among others the Lauterbrunnen guide Hilti von Allmen, the climbing journalist Guido Tonella, the head guide, stationmaster and chief policeman from Grindelwald, and John Harlin himself. Late in January Peter had asked if he could also report the climb for the *Daily Telegraph* and this was agreed.

Peter located Chris in the Pen-y-Gwryd pub in Snowdonia on the evening of 5 February. John Cleare, who was one of the cameramen for the Welsh climb, drove him to Holyhead and put him on the night sleeper to London. Late in the afternoon of Sunday 6 February, having left half his belongings scattered throughout Britain, from his cottage in Cumberland via North Wales to London, Chris got off the Jungfraubahn train at Kleine Scheidegg. He walked into the Villa Maria and John handed him a pair of skis. 'He spent the rest of the day snow-ploughing on his nose,' Dougal recalled.

Two days later the four of them decided to go on a practice climb; Dougal had never climbed with Layton before, and despite all their skiing, they were restless at their inactivity. They decided to tackle the first tower on the Eiger's

West Ridge, above Eigergletscher station. As they walked up to it the wind was getting stronger and the clouds were thickening: it was obvious that a storm was blowing up.

John started the first pitch, which followed a meandering groove through some slight overhangs. Dougal wandered off to the right and found an ice gully leading to the top of the first pitch. He cramponned up it and shouted an obscenity down to John. John had become exasperated with the iced-up holds in the groove, so he went back down and climbed up Dougal's gully. Chris and Layton followed. Some mixed climbing came next, and the last pitch was up a crack and chimney that split the top of the tower, with a long drop to the top of the Salzegg ski-run below. John and Layton climbed it easily, but as they reached the top it started to snow. Chris and Dougal had to follow in far more difficult conditions.

They had intended to climb the next tower up the ridge as well, but the snow decided them to go back down. They abseiled down some slabs into the couloir at the foot of the West Flank and tramped back through the deep snow and developing blizzard to Eigergletscher station. They were pleased with the climb; only Chris had worn gloves and their hands felt comfortable. Dougal had been climbing in Scotland for the past two months and was already very fit.

The weather during the next week was unsettled. John telephoned Geneva and Zürich airports for weather forecasts every day. He, Dougal and Layton were annoyed that the Face was no longer in the superb condition they had seen it in when they made the helicopter flight. Every fresh snowfall made it worse, although the strong winds did clear away a lot of the loose powder snow afterwards. John talked about the ten-day spell of good weather that was bound to come sooner or later. But whatever the weather, they went out skiing every day – still, as part of their conditioning for the climb, wearing no gloves.

They had never had any illusions about the problem facing them, but now that they were actually under the Face they became very much aware of all that was involved. They were particularly worried about the quantities of powder snow that were piling up on the first and theoretically easier 2,000 feet of the Face. This part of the Face was not as steep as the rest and snow tended to lodge there despite the wind.

The team of Saxons who had tried the direct in January 1963 had taken three days on this part of the route and John was reckoning on only one. But it looked as though, with their very heavy rucksacks of provisions for ten days on the Face, it could take longer. By the time they reached the immensely difficult First Band, they would be very tired from the effort of battling up to it.

But at the foot of the First Band were the windows of the Eigerwand station. Could they not use these in some way? The four Germans who made the first winter ascent of the Face in 1961 climbed it in two stages. Because of the onset of bad weather they had dumped their gear in one of the Jungfraubahn tunnel windows and then climbed back down. Six days later they went back on to the Face through the tunnel window and resumed the climb. There had been controversy over this, but this was partly because the German team did not make it clear at the time that they had used the tunnel window.

So John, Layton and Dougal decided to take their sacks up by train to the Eigerwand station and put them out into the snow below the First Band. They would be climbing the whole Face, and once they had picked up their rucksacks there would still be nine days' climbing ahead of them.

John approached the assistant stationmaster at Kleine Scheidegg, whom he knew already, to ask permission to go out of one of the Eigerwand station windows. He was referred to the stationmaster, who in turn told him to ask the director of the railway at Interlaken. The director gave his consent. The next day Chris and Dougal went up by train to the station, taking with them the three Desmaison rucksacks filled with food and bivouac equipment. They fixed a rope to one of the seats in the station and Dougal tied on to the other end and climbed out. There was a drop of 40 feet to the snow and below that the Face fell away steeply before plunging out of sight to the easier snow slopes 2,000 feet below. When Dougal was down Chris lowered the sacks to him. He dug a hole in the snow below a corner in the rock and put the sacks into it.

Dougal now had to climb back up the rope to the station. He had no Jumars,[1] so he had to go up the rope hand over hand. At the top Chris and the stationmaster hauled in furiously. Dougal reached safety very quickly and he and Chris caught the train back down to Scheidegg.

In London, Peter Gillman was sitting in the writers' room at the *Weekend Telegraph* wondering when he would be able to join the team at Kleine Scheidegg. He rang Chris nearly every day. 'Well, it could be tomorrow or the day after; it all depends on the weather,' Chris would say. As February crept on Peter became more and more restless, wishing the climb would start and afraid in case he missed the beginning.

On Monday 14 February, Chris gave a weather forecast that seemed more hopeful than usual. That was enough: Peter spent the day settling the arrangements for reporting the climb and getting film back to London, and caught the 9.30 plane to Zürich the next morning.

Meanwhile, in Switzerland, John, Layton and Dougal were out skiing. John, a superb skier, was going very fast down the Lauberhorn ski-run when he

---

1 Jumars – clamps used for prusiking. When pushed up the rope, they do not slide down again, and they have slings attached for the climber to stand in.

decided to try a *Wedel* on one leg – something he had done many times before. But this time he fell over.

He sat where he fell and Layton and Dougal skied over to him. 'My arm's out,' John said. They didn't believe him until they saw the disjointed angle of his shoulder. They couldn't tell how bad it was until he said: 'It's f—g painful.' John picked himself up, nursing his arm. Layton and Dougal skied back with him to the Villa Maria, where he sat on his bed looking utterly dejected. Layton and Dougal knew how he felt and left him without saying anything. Later on John caught the train down to Grindelwald to see a doctor.

At 5.45 that same day, 15 February, Peter stepped off the train and found the room Chris had booked for him. He wondered if the climb had begun yet, and stared rather vaguely at the Face. He found the rooms in the Villa Maria and left a note to say he had arrived. About an hour later Chris came to find him. 'Have they started yet?' Peter asked. 'You're joking,' said Chris. 'John's dislocated his shoulder.'

That evening John telephoned from Grindelwald. The doctor had ordered complete rest for five days, no skiing for ten, and no climbing for three weeks. Was this the end of the attempt already? No, said Dougal and Chris, remembering the stories of John's recoveries in the past. The day before the previous winter's attempt on the direct John had impaled his thigh on a ski-pole which had gone in up to its basket. John pulled the ski-pole out and carried on skiing so that his thigh wouldn't stiffen up. The next day he went on the Face. On the first day of his ascent of the new direct route on the south-west face of the Dru in 1965 a stone fell 1,500 feet, hit his thigh, and crushed his sciatic nerve. He cried out with pain every time he put weight on his leg, but on the third day he was leading the climb. A rescue party met him at the top and he led the descent of the whole party in a blinding snowstorm.

Next morning, 16 February, John came back: the doctor had already reduced his climbing ban from three weeks to two. The arm was very sore but John was confident that he would be able to climb again in four or five days. The greatest worry now was lest good weather should come which they wouldn't be able to use. Even so, Dougal and Layton could go ahead up the easier first third of the Face and set to work on the First Band, leaving John to follow up one or even two days later.

That evening there was a party at a girls' school in Interlaken. The school's director had invited the team, and Layton and Dougal were very keen to go. John drove them down in his micro-bus, but they evidently had a false idea of what sort of party it would be: they spent the evening drinking coffee and talking to the director. A little dispirited, they decided to drive back to Leysin that night. The Face was out of condition and it would give John a chance to rest his arm at home.

Next day, Thursday 17 February, at Scheidegg Peter and Chris went out to do the same practice climb on the West Flank that the others had done. Conditions were better for them and they were able to include the first pitch, the one that John had turned back on.

That evening in the bar they discussed the route with a picture of the Face spread out on a table. At the bar were two hardened-looking men wearing red sweaters and talking in German. As one of them passed the table he paused slightly and looked at the photograph of the Face. Peter looked up at him and he went out.

The same evening Peter and the *Weekend Telegraph* decided jointly that Peter should return to London. Next morning he packed his suitcase and caught the first train down to Lauterbrunnen.

At Leysin, John, Layton and Dougal were in the basement of the Harlins' chalet that morning, sorting through some extra equipment they thought they might need. Suddenly Marilyn Harlin burst in, panting and excited. 'A German team has started on the Face. There are eight of them.'

Layton and Dougal were flabbergasted. They knew a German team had been in training for an attempt, because they had asked John if he would join them. But a team of eight ... John appeared unmoved, but he too must have felt at least in a dilemma. 'I wouldn't be upset if someone else does it first,' he had told Peter in November. But he had already been on the route three times; and one of a climber's greatest rewards is to be able to make a first ascent. Besides, there was the possibility that because of his arm they were missing out on good climbing weather. True, the forecasts were still for unsettled weather, but the ten-day spell had to start some time. Perhaps this was it.

Peter had by now reached Zürich airport. His flight to London had just been announced when a call over the loudspeakers asked him to go to the announcements desk. A message was waiting for him: 'Opposition has started. Please phone. Bonington.' He telephoned Scheidegg but Chris was nowhere to be found. He rang the *Weekend Telegraph* and it was decided that he should come home and if necessary start again after the weekend.

The climbers left Leysin the next morning, Saturday 19 February. They parked the micro-bus at Grindelwald and as the train went up below the Eiger they saw the Germans coming down off the Face. They had climbed about 1,500 feet of the easier first third of the Face. They had fixed ropes in place as they climbed and support members of the team had hauled rucksacks up to the highest point they had reached.

That evening John, Layton and Dougal decided there was no time to lose. Layton and Dougal were to go on to the Face the next morning. Their first intention was to make a reconnaissance climb, but if the weather stayed good this could mature into a full-scale attempt.

At 3.00 a.m. on Sunday 20 February, Dougal and Layton got up. Chris had gone to the foot of the Face on Friday to take pictures of the Germans climbing – this had apparently annoyed them, for one of them threw snowballs at him whenever he came within range. But the trip had shown him the way to the foot of the Face, and he now offered to come with Dougal and Layton to show them in turn. He had been drinking with John late the previous evening and as they marched through the snow his beery breath came strongly back to them. They reached the foot of the Face in two hours.

Layton and Dougal started off up the fixed ropes the Germans had left in place, but after two pitches they decided to climb without them for practice. Above the German high point the climbing became very difficult – a 90-degree ice pitch was followed by a long snow slope with several 60-degree ice pitches. Later Jörg Lehne, co-leader of the German team, said he thought that the ice climbing on this, theoretically the easiest part of the Face, was harder than that on the north face of the Triolet on Mont Blanc, regarded as one of the most difficult snow and ice routes in the Alps.

As Dougal and Layton came near the windows of the Eigerwand station they saw rows of frightened faces peering out at them. They made their way to the rucksacks Dougal had left there two weeks earlier and dug out a platform. They took out the stove and brewed themselves a drink.

They now turned to the first great problem of the route, the forbidding First Band, the sheer, smooth cliff towering 300 feet above them. The cracks in it were thin and the rock was compact. Right from the start Layton was forced to use the subtlest of the artificial climbing techniques he had learnt on the smooth granite walls of Yosemite. The finest pitons are called knifeblades: they are just as thin, and two inches long. In places Layton could only get these one inch into the rock, but he would hang étriers[1] from them and confidently put his full weight on them. He reduced the leverage against them by using hero loops, small loops tied off on the piton against the rock instead of through the hole in the piton's head.

In four hours Layton had reached a point 90 feet up the cliff. He put in a bolt and fixed a rope from it. As it was now late in the afternoon he came back down. By now the weather was looking ominous. Black clouds were closing in and the wind was blowing up strongly. Soon it began to snow. Layton and Dougal did not feel confident enough about the lower slopes to climb down them in the gathering dark, so they prepared their bivouac. A sympathiser in the hotel kitchen had given them two pieces of steak so huge that it took half an hour to get through them.

---

1 Étriers – short ladders made either of rope with two to four aluminium rungs or of a tape sling knotted to form rungs. The climber hangs the étrier from a piton and stands up in it.

Just as they pulled their bivouac sack up around them it started to snow. Very soon they found they were bivouacked directly under an avalanche chute, and great clouds of powder snow poured over them. Their bivouac sack was too short to pull over their heads and every time an avalanche came down snow poured into the sack, which gradually filled up. It was almost impossible to sleep, but whenever one of them did doze off he gradually slid down the sloping step they were perched on, pulling the sack and the other occupant with him. When he eventually fell off the step, both of them would finish up in a jumbled heap at the bottom of the sack and have to fight their way back on to the step. By now the wind had become very strong.

Down at Scheidegg the wind was beating at the hotel. Locals were saying it was the strongest wind they had known for years, estimating that it was gusting at up to 100 mph. Chris and John were very worried about Dougal and Layton, but there was nothing they could do that night.

On the morning of Monday 21 February, the wind was still howling, driving snow swirling round the hotel. John and Chris feared Dougal and Layton might be in serious trouble, without much bivouac gear and perhaps unable to move in the storm. Chris hired a special train, costing 100 francs (about £8), to go up to the Eigerwand station, taking with him one of the Scheidegg guides and ski instructors. They arrived at the station and peered out of the window. All they could see was a rope leading down and over the edge of the snow slope below the window. Dougal and Layton had already gone.

They arrived back at Scheidegg a little shaken after the tempestuous night, but otherwise quite fit. So the first brush with the Eiger, lasting only a day, had been quite serious. It gave some indication of the problems that lay ahead: vicious weather and extreme climbing.

The storm in which Dougal and Layton retreated lasted for two more days. During this time the German team and the British–American team came together and discussed their plans for the climb. The Germans had two leaders: Peter Haag, a twenty-eight-year-old engineering student from Reutlingen; and Jörg Lehne, thirty, who worked as a progress chaser in the advertising department of the Stuttgart printing and publishing firm of Belser. The Belser company were backing the German team: they marketed news rights on the climb, and planned to produce a book at the end of it.

The other six members of the team were Karl Golikow, thirty-one, a mechanic from Stuttgart; Siegfried Hupfauer, twenty-five, a tool-maker from Ulm; Günter Schnaidt, thirty-two, a carpenter from Stuttgart; Günther Strobel, twenty-four, also a carpenter from Stuttgart; Rolf Rosenzopf, twenty-five, an engineer from Ulm; and Roland Votteler, twenty-four, a mechanic from Reutlingen. Also with the team was Harri Frey, a Swiss from Berne who worked for Belser as public relations officer. He gave out news about the team and generally acted as ground manager.

Unlike John, Dougal and Chris, none of the eight had climbed the Eiger before. But they were some of Germany's best climbers, all having good records among the classic climbs in the Alps. Jörg Lehne had been one of the party on the first great modern direct, on the north face of the Cima Grande in 1958.

Their attempt was in deadly earnest. That January, for a practice climb, four of them had traversed the Eiger, going up the Mittelegi Ridge and down the West Flank. They had a vast amount of equipment with them. But their concept of the climb was essentially different from John's. They planned a Himalayan-style rather than an Alpine assault. They would use two climbing pairs, alternating in the lead; the remaining four would haul equipment. They would fix ropes on most of the route and establish well-stocked camps at regular intervals. They would gradually push the team up the Face, climbing in good weather, retreating to their snow-holes in bad. They were reckoning on taking eighteen days on the climb, against John's ten.

The presence of two teams at Scheidegg and on the Face meant that an element of competition had been introduced. Understandably, both teams would prefer to make the first ascent. John felt that his concept of the climb was more in keeping with the spirit of alpinism, and he wanted to see his concept justified. He also felt he knew the Face better: he and Dougal had climbed it before, they had been on direct attempts on the Face before and they had probably studied the route and its problems more thoroughly than anyone else.

But there were also practical reasons why John wanted to get out ahead of the Germans on the route. His concept meant going much faster than the Germans: but if there were eight German climbers above his team, it would be extremely difficult to pass them, and his team would be slowed down to the Germans' speed. It was this that primarily worried John.

For John had always attached great value to the non-competitive aspects of climbing; by climbing with people from other countries internationalism could be fostered. At Scheidegg, even at this early stage, the possibility of the teams joining forces came to mind: the practical reason for doing so was simply that it would be very difficult to stay apart, particularly if it turned out that there was one line obviously better than any others. Already Layton and Dougal had used the ropes fixed in place by the Germans on the easier first third of the Face.

During that week of bad weather John met Jörg Lehne and Peter Haag and each outlined roughly the route they intended to take. They agreed to work together on the first third of the Face – the line which both had used already was far and away the best. But at the First Band they were on separate lines: the British–American team were attacking the First Band at its narrowest point, so that they could get on to the ice below the Second Band as quickly as possible. The Germans intended to stay on rock almost all the way to the Second Band. At the Second Band itself the British–American team would take a gully system through to the foot of the Flatiron; the Germans hoped to push a line up the rock to the right. What happened at the top of the Second Band was left vague. But there was a strong possibility that the two lines would again converge. It seemed that if John, Layton and Dougal wanted to get out in front, they were going to have to do so by that point.

Late in the week the weather improved and both teams began to think about restarting their attempts.

Then at six o'clock on the Friday of that week – 25 February – the Germans set out again. Karl Golikow and Günther Strobel reached the foot of the First Band early in the afternoon. A second pair followed them and the last four hauled equipment all day. They all bivouacked on the Face.

The next day John, Layton and Dougal had planned to return to the Face. The weather was unpromising but they set off from the bottom of the Salzegg ski-run. They had nearly reached the top of a small ridge that runs down from the Face and finishes quite close to Salzegg when they saw a large avalanche sweep the slopes below the Face, going right over several places they had to cross. They promptly changed course and ended up at Eigergletscher station, catching the train back down to Scheidegg. The Germans were unable to do any climbing that day, either.

On Sunday 27 February, Karl Golikow, seconded by Peter Haag, nailed his way up 65 feet of the First Band, while the other six brought supplies up to the *Eispalast* [the Ice Palace], the vast snow-hole they had dug themselves at the foot of the First Band.

Both the weather and the forecasts improved that day. Peter had been summoned from Inverness – where he had been working on a story about 'Winter Survival' – and flew back to Switzerland. Don Whillans also arrived. He was to climb with Chris when he went out to take photographs. The pair of them were a formidable climbing partnership. Together with Joe Brown, Don had been responsible for an immense breakthrough in the standard of rock-climbing in Britain in the 1950s. He had done most of the major alpine routes, and had been with Chris on several attempts on the Eiger. The last had ended when the two of them brought to safety the British climber Brian Nally, after his partner Barry Brewster had been killed by a fall from above the Second Icefield.

Don had also been with Chris on the first ascent of the Central Pillar of Frêney, and had been on three expeditions to the Himalaya and two to the Andes. He was a deeply rational, phlegmatic man, and Chris could have had no better person to look after him while taking photographs in precarious situations.

When Peter arrived in Chris's bedroom he found Dougal and Layton in bed, trying unsuccessfully to sleep, but at least getting some rest. They planned to leave for the Face at midnight. Their rucksacks were already packed. Tomorrow they would be back at grips with the First Band. If the good weather held, and everything went as planned, they would be on the summit in nine days' time.

# Chapter IV

The plan was that Layton, Chris and Dougal should leave for the Face soon after midnight and set to work on the First Band. John and Don would follow on the morning of Monday 28 February, carrying supplies. For the first three, this meant a dreaded early-morning start. At 2.00 a.m. they got up and dressed. Their minds had still barely grasped consciousness as they forced their unwilling bodies away from the comforts of the hotel into the exhausting knee-deep approach-march through the powder snow below the Face. The Germans' tracks had been obliterated and they changed lead constantly. It was no exhilarating upward flight in superb mountain scenery: they had to struggle unendingly to put one foot in front of the other, the snow in front of them lit only by the spot of light from their headlamps. The cold was intense and the stars unbelievably bright. They were fighting to win control of minds still longing for civilisation – if only the stars would veil over with cloud they could tell each other that bad weather was coming and go back to the hotel.

After two long hours they arrived at the cave at the foot of the fixed ropes. It was an unreal world: Dougal, shut in his own thoughts, had only a ghostly impression of Chris and Layton as their frozen fingers fumbled with their icy crampon straps. There was now no urge to linger – the cold saw to that – and they had come too far to return. In a few steps Dougal was at the bottom of the first rope. The first moves on his Jumars, before he had worked up a rhythm and was relying too much on arm strength, felt strange: he pushed up the clamps, pulled hard with his arms, and scraped for the invisible footholds with his cold feet and awkward crampons. He breathed heavily between moves, resting in his safety sling. But he began to remember the well-practised movements and soon all three were moving smoothly up the ropes.

In two hours Layton and Dougal reached the foot of the First Band. They had been climbing with such concentration that they had hardly noticed night become day. Chris had fallen behind to take photographs, so Layton and Dougal went over to the German snow-hole to say good morning. Peter Haag greeted them with hot coffee and they spent a pleasant quarter of an hour talking with him, Karl Golikow and Günther Strobel about the difficulties ahead. Layton and Dougal were much impressed with the comfort the Germans were living in, particularly when they remembered their own last atrocious bivouac. Chris arrived, and they decided that when he had taken all the pictures he wanted Chris should ask Peter Haag to lend him a shovel so that he could dig a snow-hole of their own.

Dougal and Layton now set to work on the First Band. Dougal prusiked[1] up to the previous high point and sat swinging comfortably in slings. Layton came up and climbed over his head. Above the stance was a spider's web of blind cracks that was going to need artificial climbing of a very high standard. Dougal sat and watched as Layton moved and placed pitons with precision and speed. Dougal had done many of the major artificial routes in the Alps, but never before had he seen anything approaching Layton's skill. In three hours Layton came to the end of his run-out, fixed an expansion bolt for a belay, and sat there swinging in his slings.

Dougal started up after him, taking out the pitons. At once his feeling about the difficulty of the pitch was confirmed. A European climber would have littered the rock with bolts, but Layton had not used one. (Not once during the whole climb did Layton, John and Dougal use a bolt for direct aid; they used them only for belays.)

The climbing so held their attention that it was some time before they were really aware that it had started to snow. This was serious: they knew that powder-snow avalanches were going to start almost at once. Dougal was half-way up the pitch when suddenly everything became dark. This was the warning that he would be deluged by powder snow in just ten seconds' time. He dropped his hammer, slumped in his étriers, and tried to curl up as small as possible. When the avalanche arrived he felt as though he was being immersed in a waterfall.

Above him Layton was having the same trouble. In his stance there was nothing he could do except bend his head. To make matters worse, they could hardly communicate with each other. Whenever Dougal opened his mouth to shout, it was filled with snow. Down at Scheidegg Peter was feeling for them: he had looked through the telescope at lunchtime and seen three huge avalanches submerge them in ten minutes. The Germans' line to the right was less exposed but they too were suffering.

Dougal struggled up until he was just below Layton and then they decided they had both had enough. But retreat was easier said than done. Dougal was hanging in Jumars on one rope and had to transfer to an abseil position on the other. To do this he needed bare hands, and he really felt the cold. He thought he had changed over successfully and started on the long free abseil down. He was about 100 feet above the snow when suddenly he stopped dead and flipped upside down. This made him let go of the abseil rope – normally a fatal move.

---

1 Prusik – a method of moving up a fixed rope, using either a pair of slings tied round the rope with a prusik knot or a pair of Jumar or Heibler clamps. The clamps or slings slide up the rope when the climber pushes them but do not slip down again. The climber stands in the knotted slings or in a pair of slings attached to the clamps.

But he had jammed because he was still attached to the other rope and it was this that now stopped him from falling. He quickly clipped a Jumar on to the abseil rope to safeguard his position. But he was not out of trouble yet. Avalanches were constantly pouring over his head and the other rope was still wound round his thigh and caught in his seat-sling. He simply could not move downwards. He tried pulling up on his Jumars and somersaulting on the rope, but this did not help. The avalanches came down unrelentingly, and higher up Layton was beginning to get worried. Dougal thought it was a strange place to have to spend the rest of his life.

There was only one solution: a knife. The problem now was to get hold of one. Chris was down below at the foot of the cliff so Dougal shouted down to him. 'Go and ask the Germans for a knife, tie it on to the rope and send it up, urgently – I'm hanging free.' Chris wandered off and disappeared into the German snow-hole; Dougal swung gently to and fro in the incessant avalanches, and higher up Layton was being inundated too. About twenty minutes later Chris came back with a knife. He tied it on to the rope and at last Dougal could pull it up. He had a long fumble with frozen fingers to untie the little package on which his life now virtually depended, but at last he cut the abseil rope and twanged violently on to the other one. He descended gratefully to the snow. Layton followed him, shaken and shivering, and said he wanted to go back to Scheidegg. Chris and Dougal decided to stay up and enlarge the snow-hole Chris had been working on that morning.

In the meantime John and Don were running into difficulties too. They had left Scheidegg at 9.30 that morning with the loads they were going to carry up to the First Band. But by the time they reached the foot of the fixed ropes the avalanches were pouring down the Face. They gallantly started up the ropes, but soon realised that things were impossible. 'It wasn't really too good up there,' John said when he got back to Scheidegg.

Chris and Dougal spent the evening working on their snow-hole 100 feet to the left of the Germans. Chris had borrowed a shovel from Peter Haag and also told Peter how comfortable his snow-hole looked. Next morning the Swiss paper *Blick*, in a front-page report headlined 'Sprint up the Eiger', told how badly equipped the British–American team were and how they had asked to share the German snow-hole. *Blick* emphasised the competitive element of the climb; a picture of John, Dougal and Layton was captioned 'Against the Germans'. But from the first the climbers were always very friendly when they met and it became quite normal for them to lend each other pieces of equipment.

Chris and Dougal had a good night, though a rather cramped one. When they looked out on the morning of Tuesday 1 March, they found that it had snowed heavily in the night. Gigantic spindrift[1] avalanches were pouring down the Face, huge boiling clouds of snow that sometimes covered as much as a third of the Face at once. At Scheidegg, John said they were the biggest he had ever seen on the Eiger. Climbing was obviously out of the question, so Chris and Dougal decided to enlarge the snow-hole further. At this stage it was just a question of providing somewhere to spend a dry night. They brewed up first and then set to work. They dug all morning and stopped when it seemed that the roof might cave in if someone accidentally pushed his shovel through it. By now it was big enough for anyone – except Layton – to stand up in, and there was room for three people to sleep in it at night.

At lunchtime the avalanches were still coming down and it looked as though it might snow as well, so Dougal and Chris decided to go back to Scheidegg. At 2.00 p.m. they set off down the Face, going very cautiously: they didn't know if the snow on it was compact and would hold. The fixed ropes were still badly placed: a single 600-foot length hung down from the Eigerwand station window, and at the bottom they had to pendulum on it to get to the right stance. By now it was snowing and they were being continually deluged by clouds of spindrift coming down from the Face. At the bottom of the fixed ropes they decided, because of the avalanche risk, to go straight down to Alpiglen immediately below them, instead of crossing below the Face. Above them Peter Haag and Günther Strobel stayed in their snow-hole all day.

That evening at Scheidegg John and Layton decided to go back to the Face the next morning. It would be John's first day on the Face since he had dislocated his shoulder and he was anxious to see if it would stand up to the climbing.

The morning of Wednesday 2 March dawned perfectly and John and Layton used the Salzegg ski-lift to go up to the foot of the West Flank. They skied across high up under the Face to the bottom of the fixed ropes, and reached the snow-hole at the foot of the First Band at 2.30 p.m. Peter Haag and Günther Strobel were already on the First Band and had climbed another 80 feet.

But John and Layton didn't start themselves – and this was the result of a definite and significant policy decision and the precise moment of the first modification of the Alpine concept of the climb. The weather had been unsettled for two weeks already, and the forecasts still gave no hope of continuous clear weather ahead. 'The weather for the type of assault we had planned has not been good at all,' explained John in a radio call from the Face. 'Instead of the settled air mass weather normal in winter time we have had a steady generation of air mass storms, from Föhn storms to associated frontal system storms.'

---

1  Spindrift – powder snow blown in the wind or falling as an avalanche.

If they continued to wait at Scheidegg for the promise of ten days of good weather they might never get off the ground: and the Germans had already taken advantage of their own snow-hole to continue their attack on the First Band the moment conditions had allowed. So the team decided to use their snow-hole as a camp from which to launch attacks on the Face. In addition, they ordered extra food, clothing and bivouac equipment for the different kind of assault they now planned. They intended to remain faithful to their original Alpine concept as soon as the weather allowed. 'If we have a good spell of weather in prospect, we'll continue our Alpine tactics and make a single summit push from wherever our high point is at that time,' John said. This could possibly be from as low down on the Face as the snow-cave they were now making at the foot of the First Band – they had already prepared the First Band, and on the original Alpine schedule they could reach the summit in seven days from there. More realistically, they could aim to get to the Death Bivouac in the present spell of good weather, establish a good camp there, and use that as their blasting-off point for the summit.

So that afternoon Layton and John continued to enlarge the hole so that it could accommodate four people. At the same time Peter Haag, seconded by Günther Strobel, was edging his way up to the line of cracks and chimneys about 100 feet to the right of Layton's line. The British–American route attacked the cliff at its lowest point, where it was about 250 feet high. Above the cliff they would get into a system of ice gullies that led to the foot of the Second Band – these, they reckoned, would go quickly. But Jörg Lehne had said he thought they were impossible, and the Germans intended to follow a line on rock to the right that would take them almost to the foot of the Second Band.

Late that afternoon Peter Haag was about 250 feet up the Band, having climbed 120 feet in the day, when he came to an overhang. There was only a poor crack where he wanted to put his piton, so he banged three in together. He hung his étrier from them and stood up in it – only to fall 30 feet before being held by the rope. He bruised his back and wrist and cut his finger, so he retreated to the foot of the Band. There he met Jörg Lehne and Günter Schnaidt, who had arrived at the First Band that afternoon, an hour after Layton and John.

Down at Kleine Scheidegg Peter had been organising the press coverage of the climb. The *Daily Telegraph*, for whom he was doing daily reports, had asked for as many pictures as possible. This meant that someone had to drive to Zürich airport with the rolls of exposed film each day. John had produced from the Leysin community a cheerful Canadian girl, Joan Matthews. Wednesday was the second time she had gone off to Zürich. At 7.00 p.m. she telephoned Scheidegg. 'Er, Peter,' she said, and then, after a pause, 'I hope you insured the car for me because you're going to need it because I was overtaking this other car and it moved out and I drove off the road and broke the fence and I don't think the car will go any more.' When Peter had calmed her down it emerged that she had driven off the road at 60 mph, wrecked the car completely, and clambered out of the wreckage with a scratched little finger.

Dougal decided to ski down to console her. With John's dislocated shoulder, the crash was the second bad accident in a fortnight. Don looked at Dougal as he strapped on his skis in the darkness outside. In a voice of doom he said: 'Accidents always go in threes. Yer'll break yer bluddy leg.' But Dougal got down to Grindelwald in twenty minutes – and in one piece.

After this episode it was decided that one girl by herself was not up to hair-raising dashes to Zürich and back in a day. Chris Bonington flew his wife Wendy over from England to help. Also on hand in Scheidegg was Marie-France Rivière, a camp-follower from Paris, who had arrived soon after the first attempt on the First Band. Besides transporting film, the three girls also helped with weather forecasts and radio calls to the Face.

The spell of good weather was still with the team the next morning, Thursday 3 March. Dougal and Joan came back to Scheidegg by an early train, bringing with them the extra equipment Joan had picked up from Max Eiselin's shop in Lucerne. Dougal, Chris and Don were going to the foot of the Face with supplies and it was planned – though rather vaguely – that Chris and Dougal would go up the fixed ropes to take over from John and Layton.

John and Layton had started climbing early that morning, at 7.30. By mid-morning the First Band, the route's first great problem, had been overcome. Layton went up the fixed ropes first and then climbed a short pitch of 50 feet to the top. John then moved past Layton and led up the steep ice gully that went to the right towards a gully system that appeared to penetrate the Second Band, about 250 feet higher up. After 80 feet of climbing on steep, thin ice, John fixed the rope and came back down to Layton's stance. The two decided to spend the rest of the day improving the fixed rope on the First Band. It was a 300-foot length of 7-millimetre perlon and the prusik up it was almost entirely free: Layton had noticed that it was already wearing in places. He and John put another 7-millimetre length next to it so that they would be able to prusik up a double rope.

To their right, Jörg Lehne had led past the overhang where Peter Haag had fallen the day before and was making for a large recess in the face that was an obvious bivouac site. Peter Haag was spending the day resting in bed in his snow-hole after his fall.

Dougal, Don and Chris had by now battled their way to the foot of the fixed ropes carrying 60-pound packs, loaded mostly with food and new rope. Dougal led all the way – Don appeared to be coughing up his guts and Chris was as usual late in leaving.

The vague intention Chris and Dougal had had of replacing John and Layton did not materialise. They decided that John and Layton would probably stay up in the snow-hole that night, so they started back to Scheidegg. Late in the afternoon John finished fixing the rope and went back down to the snow-hole ready to prepare for the night; to the right Jörg Lehne was coming back down too, having failed by 30 feet to reach the new bivouac site when he ran out of rope. When John got inside the snow-hole he found Layton feverishly packing his rucksack. 'If we don't hurry up we won't get back,' he thrust at John as he came in.

'There was a certain amount of high cirrus about and that's always a sign of bad weather,' John explained to Dougal and Chris at Scheidegg some two hours later. 'Anyway, I thought you were going to replace us.' John was elated because his shoulder had stood up to the day's climbing, and his sense of well-being merged into one of his customary moods of optimism about the route as a whole. After their arduous day carrying supplies Chris and Dougal were less excited. Peter missed these nuances of feeling. It was his birthday, and he was busy eating a whole roast chicken.

Laden with guilt at not having replaced John and Layton the previous day, Chris and Dougal left Scheidegg at 2.30 a.m. on Friday, 4 March, to make a push for the Second Band. They carried heavy rucksacks again, but fortunately the tracks they had made the day before were still there to follow. By the time Peter looked through the telescope after breakfast Dougal was at the top of the First Band. 'They're climbing already – great!' he told the others. Later that morning he went to look again, expecting to find Chris and Dougal working their way up the gully system leading to the Second Band. But by this time Dougal was standing at the foot of the First Band and Chris was 1,000 feet below him, half-way down the easier part of the Face. 'We dropped a pair of Jumar clamps through a misunderstanding,' Chris explained later. Dougal had taken a 300-foot rope up to the top of the First Band for hauling supplies. He had told Chris to fix down the end of it, but somehow this instruction had got lost between comprehension and execution. Dougal had put the Jumar clamps on the rope and let them go. They slid down the rope, shot off the end and tumbled and bounced half-way down the rest of the Face. Dougal had also dropped Wendy Bonington's camera – it was probably pulled off his wrist on the way up. To add to his feeling of discouragement, several spindrift avalanches poured over his head and a few wisps of cloud appeared in the sky. He took advantage of a sudden moment of indecision to go back down the fixed ropes. Chris came back up waving the Jumars, and to cheer themselves they went into the snow-cave for a brew-up.

After a drink of tea they decided to go back down to the foot of the Face to get the supplies they and Don had left there the previous day. On the way down they met John and Layton. Chris turned round and went back up with them, but Dougal carried on down. In the cave at the bottom he picked up a rucksack full of food and went back up the ropes. It took him only an hour and he was pleased at how fit he was becoming. Late that afternoon Layton hauled four heavy rucksacks to the top of the First Band, which showed how fit he was already.

In the snow-cave that evening the four climbers laid plans for a big push the next day. Layton and Chris were to carry more rucksacks to the top of the First Band while John and Dougal pushed on as far as they could – certainly to the foot of the Second Band, and with luck a good part of the way up it as well. The German team had spent the day consolidating their position, too. Peter Haag had led into the rock recess that Jörg Lehne had failed to reach the previous day, and they had spent the whole day digging out a bivouac site there and hauling up supplies. It was obvious that they too were preparing for a big push.

On the morning of Saturday 5 March came the anticlimax. It started to snow in the night and by the time Peter went outside to make the 7.45 radio call six inches had fallen at Scheidegg. The four men jammed into the snow-hole had had a bad night, having to get up continually to fight off the spindrift blowing in through chinks in the entrance covering. Because of their exertions they overslept the call-time by twenty-five minutes. The weather forecast Peter gave them said that it would snow for the next two days. No one could see the Face – it was hidden from Scheidegg by cloud, and the climbers were still in their hole – but it was almost certain that spindrift avalanches would as usual be pouring down.

The team decided that it would be best if Layton and Chris went back to Scheidegg and John and Dougal stayed in the hole. If there was no climbing to be done, two of them might just as well wait for good weather in comfort. Like the Germans, John and Dougal would be ready to climb again as soon as conditions allowed. Chris and Layton would then go back to the Face to support them by hauling rucksacks and organising supplies.

Layton disappeared down the fixed ropes towards Scheidegg and civilisation at 10.15 and Chris followed an hour later. It was the first time that either John or Dougal had been forced to spend a completely inactive day in a snow-hole on a mountain.

But they found there was too much to do to be bored. What occupied most time was their continual battle to clear away the powder snow that came in past the entrance. This settled on their sleeping bags like some innocuous powder, and Dougal felt he wanted to ignore it. But it was anything but innocuous, because if left there it would make the sleeping bag damper and damper. The bag would then freeze into uselessness. So they would heave themselves up from their lying position, brush every last grain of snow off their sleeping bags, and then slump back. A quarter of an hour later there would be a swishing noise, a surging upthrust of snow at the entrance, and everything would be covered again. They also spent a lot of the time trying to stop the spindrift coming into the hole in the first place. They jammed socks into the small holes around the entrance and between the roof of snow and back wall of rock. The large holes they tried to block with the canvas mailbags in which they had brought up some of their gear. They were also kept busy cooking their meals and making the regular radio calls to Scheidegg.

Despite these interminable tasks, the bivouac was a good one. Instead of being perched on a ledge in the open, they were more or less protected from the elements. And because of their down sleeping bags and foam mattresses there was no physical discomfort.

At lunchtime Karl Golikow, Rolf Rosenzopf, Roland Votteler and Siegfried Hupfauer arrived at the top of the fixed ropes. As they stumped past the snow-hole each one pushed his head past the entrance canopy to greet their rivals and fellow-climbers. Rolf Rosenzopf, the last of the four, gave them a huge grin. The journey up to their own bivouac was all the Germans were able to do that day, either. Jörg Lehne and Günter Schnaidt had wanted to go up to their second bivouac to join Peter Haag and Günther Strobel, but they had to content themselves with passing messages between the two snow-holes on a piece of 3-millimetre nylon.

Saturday's snow gave way to good weather again on Sunday 6 March. John and Dougal came out of their snow-hole to see a magnificent morning, with clear skies above and a few wisps of mist in the valley below. It certainly didn't look as though it would snow and the spindrift avalanches coming down seemed to be at an acceptable minimum, so they got ready to climb. Dougal jumared up to the top of the fixed ropes first. He had with him an empty rucksack which he half-filled from one of the packs that Chris and Layton had left there two days earlier. As leader, it was his privilege to climb light. John prusiked up to join him and Dougal made his way up to the previous high point while John belayed him.

Dougal had hoped that the climbing was going to ease, but as soon as he left the security of the fixed ropes he realised how difficult it still was. He was on crackless slabs plated over with ice and he could arrange no protection. To add to his difficulties, he had clipped into too many pitons on the previous section and there was severe rope drag. He would pull up on to a small ice nick with only the front points of his crampons gripping, to be brought to a sudden halt in mid-movement by the pull of the rope behind him. There were many hard moves on the first pitch, and after being nearly pulled off several times he started to pull up enough rope for each move first before embarking on it. The pitch took a long time and the lack of protection meant continuous tension: Dougal was very thankful when at last he reached a reasonable belay stance.

But even here there were problems: the cracks were still poor and he banged in a spider's web of seven pitons before telling John to prusik up.

Just round the corner from the stance the Germans were hauling loads up to their second bivouac. Karl Golikow was prancing around like a clown, acting as cheer-leader. 'It's a very hard life,' he shouted in reply to Dougal's greeting. Above him Peter Haag and Günther Strobel were working their way up rock towards the foot of the Second Band.

John arrived at the stance and Karl's words became true. A pitch of only 50 feet led to the easier snowfield between the First and Second Bands. But the ice was thin, protection still poor, and the angle was an unrelenting 80 degrees. Just swinging his axe threatened to dislodge Dougal as he held on precariously with fingertips and crampon points. But finally he came out on to a beautiful 50-degree snow slope and belayed.

John followed him up and led through. The snow was firm and John climbed quickly. But by now it was getting dark and they still had to find a place to bivouac. John took a full 140-foot run-out and stuck his axe into a bulge of snow under a rock overhang. The axe disappeared up to his hand. He enlarged the hole he had made and discovered a natural snow-cave into which he disappeared, to give a jubilant yell from inside. Dougal followed up the pitch and joined John in the hole. It didn't need much enlarging and they were soon brewing up. They were happy with the day's progress and even happier with what they had seen of the route through the Second Band: it looked less difficult than they had feared.

Things had been happening that day on the Scheidegg–Eiger trail as well. Independent Television News had come out from London on Saturday 5 March, and wanted to make the long slog from the hotel to the foot of the face to film authentic interviews with the climbers. Alan Hankinson, the reporter, had with him a Dutch cameraman and sound recordist who had never been on a mountain before in their lives. They had with them 16-millimetre and 35-millimetre cameras, sound-recording equipment and a vast tripod. Two American dentists from John's old USAF base at Hahn, Cleve McCarty and Bill Chipman, gave a hand.

Layton was returning to the Face and Don and Chris were to carry rucksacks full of supplies up to the foot of the First Band. Peter came for the ride and Layton sent him on ahead to break trail.

Large sections of the slopes below the Face had avalanched the previous night and Peter was a little apprehensive as he ploughed thigh-deep through the tumbled snow debris. 'Get buried in that lot and they wouldn't find you till spring,' Layton said to cheer him up. Chris and Don followed a short way behind, and strung out across the slopes came the ITN men and their helpers. Dougal, from his belay stance, wondered whether it was some new mass onslaught on the Face. Finally all nine men reached the cave at the foot of the fixed ropes and the cameras were set up. Layton recorded first, explaining about the problems of the climb, and in particular how they had been plagued with bad weather for two weeks.

Then it was Don's turn. 'Say a few nice things, Don,' pleaded Layton.

'Do you mind being a porter?' Alan Hankinson asked. 'No – it suits me fine,' said Don, 'because I don't have to go any higher.'

'How many times have you made it up to the bivouac cave?'

'I made it half-way, once.'

'No, how many times have you been to the bivouac cave?'

'That's right, I've been up once, half-way.'

Don was asked if he thought there was a race on between the teams.

'If it's a race, it's the slowest race in the world.'

Chris Bonington was the third to be interviewed.

'What do you say to the criticisms that the climb's being done for the money?' asked Hankinson.

'No one does a climb like this just for the money,' said Chris. 'But doing this kind of climb is an extremely expensive thing. So unless you're a rich person you've got to find the money from somewhere, and this is what John Harlin and the Germans have done – they want to go on the climb and they've both found sponsors to make the thing possible.'

He too was asked if he thought the two teams were trying to race each other to the top.

'They both made their plans completely independently of the other party, and it's just an unfortunate coincidence that they arrived at the foot of the climb at the same time. Once they're there, I think one's got to be realistic. Each party would like the satisfaction of making the first ascent. But I think the race aspect is being whipped up by the Press. On the Face you get things into perspective, and there's a definite feeling of friendship and co-operation between the two parties.'

After the interviews the cameraman was helped to the foot of the first fixed rope to film Don pulling himself up on his Jumars. Layton had disappeared up the rope already and Chris soon followed. The television crew left the cave and made their way back to Scheidegg in easy stages.

Meanwhile, back on the fixed ropes, Don was in trouble. He was three pitches below the First Band when he kicked into the ice so hard that one of his crampons flew off. 'I knew if I borrowed someone else's gear I'd be in trouble.' He bent down to secure the strap and then one of his Jumar clamps came off the rope. 'I looked down and suddenly the ground swung around all over the place. I got an overhand knot into that rope in about half a second.' The unfortunate Don had encountered an old enemy of his – an attack of vertigo – that had ruined at least one major expedition for him in the past. He had to leave his sack where it was and go back down the rope. He tramped impassively back along the track to Scheidegg, wearing his dark glasses and smoking. 'Il est formidable, le Don,' said Harri Frey, watching him through the telescope at the hotel.

Chris followed Don across the slopes to Scheidegg later. Layton stayed in the bivouac at the bottom of the First Band. At Scheidegg no one knew what had been happening on the Face after midday because clouds had come up from the valley and hidden it. The first intimation Peter had of the day's good progress was when Layton radioed at 6.45 that Dougal and John had not come back to the snow-hole. As far as he knew, the next good bivouac site was near the foot of the Second Band. His surmise was correct.

John and Dougal had a cold but comfortable night, and on the morning of Monday 7 March the weather was still clear. Chris left Scheidegg again for the Face and John and Dougal left their snow-hole. As always, it was a pleasure for the climbers to start moving slowly upwards. Dougal cramponned up the crisp, firm snow, lost in wonderment at his savage environment. He delighted in the controlled coordination of mind and muscle on the greatest face in Europe. For him, this was the essence of climbing. He reached a belay stance and shouted 'Good morning, Charlie' to Karl Golikow, already at work on the wall to Dougal's right. Karl replied with his usual greeting: 'It's a hard life.' It certainly was: a moment later there was a great scraping of crampons as Karl fell 30 feet into the snow below him. Dougal was anxious for him, but he picked himself up from the snow muttering to himself and grinning.

The fall appeared to cause the Germans to change their minds about the line they were following on the rock to the right of the British–American route: they now started to traverse left to the gully system that John and Dougal were heading for. Dougal led to its foot and brought John up just as Jörg and Karl arrived. The two pairs talked together and decided to follow the same route as far as necessary, but climbing as two separate ropes. John set off up the left-hand side of the snow-filled chimney and Jörg kept to the rock on the right. The chimney led to a series of ledges that in turn led to the top of the Second Band. John and Dougal were fixing ropes for Chris and Layton, now only a short way behind with heavy loads.

The two teams carried on up the steep ice gully, reaching the top in three pitches each. They were now faced with a problem. To break through to the ledge system they had to climb either a steep snow-filled chimney or a rotten wall to its right. John and Dougal chose the chimney, Karl and Jörg the wall.

Dougal and Karl stood on the same tiny stance, belayed to the same expansion bolt, taking mock-bets on the two leaders. Both routes were difficult and John arrived at the top about ten minutes before Jörg. 'You owe me a beer,' Dougal told Karl as he moved off to second the pitch, reflecting that this was the bitter rivalry in action. When he got on to the pitch he found just how hard it had been – the main problem was the unstable snow. When he reached John's stance Jörg Lehne pushed a bar of chocolate into his mouth, particularly welcome as he and John hadn't eaten anything since early that morning. Karl arrived shortly afterwards, a little fed up because one of the pitons he was on had come out and he had been left dangling on the rope.

From Scheidegg Peter had watched through the telescope the two pairs climbing alongside one another. It was the closest they had been during the climb. 'British–American team takes 15-foot lead in Eiger climb,' he wrote, tongue-in-cheek, in his report that night.

By now dusk was gathering and Karl and Jörg decided to abseil back down to the higher of the two German snow-holes. But Dougal and John wanted to get to the top of the Band. There was still a difficult traverse pitch to make and Dougal led off in the semi-darkness.

A fantastic sight awaited him at the top of the Band. The cloud-ceiling had crept up to 400 feet below them. The sun was setting in a deep red blaze, inflaming the neighbouring Oberland peaks. Dougal stood in the perfect stillness and intense cold and watched the sun slip away. The Face seemed tough and sinister in the twilight, and he felt oppressively aware of the immense problem facing him.

John was battling across the traverse in almost complete darkness and his arrival brought one immediate problem home to Dougal: they had no snow-cave in which to spend the night. After four hours of searching and digging they still didn't have one, and finally had to make do with a platform they cut into the ice. It had been a hard day and at midnight, in bitter cold, they pitched their tent. They had no solid food left: this was in the rucksacks that Layton and Chris, sleeping below them in the second bivouac cave, would be bringing up in the morning. But they had enough to make themselves hot drinks; with these they passed away the night until finally they fell asleep.

Tuesday 8 March saw the third perfect dawn in succession, a run of good weather unprecedented on the climb so far. Dougal and John were very weary after spending so long setting up their bivouac, but they staggered out of their tent to prepare for the day's climbing. Karl Golikow came cheerily up the ropes towards them. Fifteen feet from them he stumbled, pushing his ice-axe into a bulge of snow. The axe disappeared, just as John's had two nights before. Karl had found a perfect natural ice-cave, which he promptly entered and claimed as German territory. John and Dougal felt a little sick.

Nothing daunted, however, they sorted out their climbing gear at the foot of the steep ice gully leading to the top of the Second Band. Dougal was just tying on the rope ready to start climbing when Günther Strobel came round the corner, blandly said, 'Good morning', and set off up the gully.

John and Dougal began to realise it was not their day and decided to take new stock of their position. After the previous day's excitements, their equipment was badly organised. They had no solid food with them and the ropes and pitons they would need for a push were below with Chris and Layton. Dougal went and had a look at another possible line, but it started up a chimney that was blocked with a mass of corniced snow, so they decided to spend the day organising their equipment for a fast push the next day. They accepted Peter Haag's offer to take a rope for them to the top of the ice gully leading out of the Second Band. They then started to dig out a hole for the four of them to bivouac in that night – extremely hard work as they were digging into ice. Layton and Chris arrived with the first of the heavy rucksacks and then went back down for more. They brought all the heavy rucksacks to the high point that day, an impressive feat. Then they began to organise the supplies into five loads for the push up the Death Bivouac.

All morning down at Scheidegg there had been elation in the German camp and puzzlement in the British–American one. As far as could be seen, Peter Haag and Günther Strobel had climbed quickly to the top of the Second Band while John and Dougal had turned back from their line. Peter and Günther were now traversing below the Flatiron into the Second Icefield. The British–American camp waited anxiously for John and Dougal to follow them. The midday radio call was hardly explicit: John just said they had decided to spend that day organising.

In the afternoon Peter Haag and Günther Strobel pressed on strongly up the Second Icefield without fixing ropes. They reached the top of the Icefield late in the afternoon and tried to climb the band of rock dividing it from the traverse line to the Death Bivouac. They failed in their first attempt and moved several hundred feet to the right to the steep pitch of grade V used on the normal route. By now it was getting dark, so they did not try it that night, bivouacking just beneath it.

The British–American team were having bivouac troubles of their own. John and Dougal had hacked at the ice all afternoon but the cave they had dug out was hardly big enough for the four of them. Fortunately, it occurred to them that some more supplies would be useful – and who better to fetch them than Layton, the largest man in the party, and also the most restless away from civilisation? It took him one-and-three-quarter hours to descend from the top of the Second Band to Kleine Scheidegg. He carried with him a list of what was wanted: candles, gloves, karabiners, radio batteries and chocolate. Wednesday was to be the day of the big push to the Death Bivouac. Snow was forecast for Thursday and the team felt that if they could set up a camp there they would have a good forward position when the bad weather came. But there were 800 feet of climbing from the Second Band. It was going to be a hard day.

Layton left Scheidegg at 2.00 a.m. on Wednesday 9 March, and reached the bivouac near the top of the Second Band by the time John and Dougal were ready to set out. Carrying heavy loads, they prusiked up the rope left by the Germans to the top of the Second Band. Here they were faced with a decision about their route. Originally they had thought of taking a line to the left of the Flatiron that would lead eventually to the foot of the Third Icefield. But immediately in front of them was a confused system of gullies and chimneys, and the climbing looked very hard. The alternative was to go the way Peter Haag and Günther Strobel had taken the previous day: traverse below the Flatiron and directly up the Second Icefield. This was a possibility they had always had in mind: in the fold-out picture of the face in Peter's copy of *The White Spider*, for example, John had marked the left-hand route in a continuous line and the right-hand route – the one the Germans had taken – with dots. The progress the Germans had made the day before decided it for them: the right-hand route was clear and straightforward and could obviously be climbed without major difficulties.

Dougal led across the traverse below the Flatiron and into the Second Icefield. The climbing was ideal: for the first time the Eiger seemed almost friendly. The Germans' marks had been obliterated and the hard snow-ice meant calf-straining pitches, but Dougal was feeling so fit that he could almost relax. They fixed ropes in the difficult places for Chris and Layton, following up with the heavy rucksacks. Below Chris and Layton two German climbers, also hauling supplies, followed.

Dougal front-pointed[1] to the top of the Second Icefield, thinking of the previous times he had been there. Even though it was winter, he felt happier and more relaxed than at any time on the normal route.

But the Eiger soon jolted him from this growing sense of security. As they started on the difficult pitch up the rock band at the top of the Second Icefield, the one taken by climbers on the normal route, a film of grey cloud began to spread over the sky. John led the pitch, using the pitons left in place by climbers over the years.

They led alternately from there to the German high point 300 feet from the crest of the Flatiron. It was threatening to snow. Peter Haag and Günther Strobel were furiously digging a snow-hole. John and Dougal were now very tired; they had been carrying heavy rucksacks all day and they had again had no food since the morning. As Layton and Chris came up the ropes and joined them on their stance it was getting dark and the snow had now begun.

But they were still determined to reach the Death Bivouac. Dougal took off his rucksack, tied on to a 100-metre rope, and set off on the difficult traverse.

---

1 Front-point – to climb ice standing on only the two projecting front points of one's crampons, needing strong calves and good balance.

Despite his tiredness, it was a delight to move unladen; he moved fast on his crampons, swinging his axe to cut steps with his left hand and using his ice-dagger as well. It was classic hard ice-climbing. But the protection was almost non-existent and in 300 feet he only managed to place one poor ice-screw and one good Chromolly piton. By the time he reached the Death Bivouac it was snowing hard. As soon as he arrived he looked for a place to dig a snow-hole. A little above him, through the darkness and driving snow, loomed a large snow bulge. He attacked it like a madman.

One by one John, Chris and Layton arrived, carrying one rucksack each. This meant that two sacks were still at the other end of the traverse. In an increasing blizzard the four worked on the snow-hole in shifts, one digging from above, one from below. Only one headlamp worked properly: on the other, someone had to hold the wires on to the terminals, which meant taking it in turns to suffer frozen fingers. At midnight, after four hours' digging, the snow-hole was big enough for the four of them to squeeze inside.

But there were still the two packs 300 feet away in the darkness and driving snow at the other end of a most difficult traverse – and one of them contained the brewing gear. Chris said he'd only come to take photographs, Layton was worried about his feet, which had got rather cold. So Dougal stumped off into the night. It was the wildest traverse he had ever made. The snow drove into his face and he could see only a few yards ahead by his headlight. He had clipped into the rope he had fixed himself, but it was no use for following the route because of the slack in it. He strayed on to some snow-covered slabs and, inevitably, slipped, slithering 30 feet towards the drop to the Second Icefield before being pulled up by the rope, now at full stretch – and he knew that the anchors holding the rope at each end were not particularly good. He used his Heibler clamp to climb back up the rope to the next anchor point. It was the shaky ice-screw. He gave it a pull and it came out of its hole in his hand. He replaced it with his ice-dagger and tightened up the rope.

He pressed on, finding the traverse not quite so wild and rather more secure. He called in at the German snow-hole to say hello. Peter Haag gave him some cigarettes for Layton – the only one of the three to smoke. Jörg Lehne, crouching over a stove, said 'Salut, Dougal,' non-committal as usual.

At last Dougal reached the rucksacks. He found the one containing the brewing gear and set off back. The traverse went more quickly this time – at least he didn't fall off. He savoured the idea of climbing on the Eiger in the dark and in a storm. When he got back he found the others huddled together waiting for him. John, anxious, had been shouting into the night. But time had not been important to Dougal: he had been in a small but self-sufficient world of his own.

John now left to fetch the other rucksack. He too enjoyed the traverse, particularly now that Dougal had secured the rope. He paid an early-morning social call on the four Germans crammed into their hole and arrived back safely at the Death Bivouac an hour after leaving.

The night's excitements were not yet over. The snow-hole was lit by a candle. During the brewing-up Dougal started to change a gas-cylinder which he thought was empty. He was wrong. There was a hiss of gas and the cylinder became a blazing mass of flame. Dougal's one thought was to throw it out of the snow-hole before it exploded. He made a brave attempt but missed. At the same time Chris dived for the entrance. 'It must be his tank training,' Dougal thought, as he saw him disappear. Luckily, Chris remembered where he was just in time to prevent himself plunging over the edge of the 4,000-foot drop and stopped, more in the hole than out. John grabbed the still blazing gas-cylinder and hurled it past him into the void. Chris pulled himself sheepishly back into the hole and John muttered darkly about 'inappropriate behaviour'. The brewing-up continued. No one could find the legs to the paraffin stove and Dougal had to sit immobile, holding the stove between his knees and the pot of melting snow in his hands. Layton was curved in a U-shape in the centre of the hole and the other three were jammed between him and the snow walls. Finally, some time between 3.00 and 4.00 a.m., they got tired of brewing hot drinks, and one by one fell asleep.

# Chapter V

They woke up late the next morning, 10 March, missing the 7.45 radio call. When they looked outside the snow-hole they found it had stopped snowing. But there could be no question of climbing for the moment. They were worn out after the previous night and the cave was in chaos.

They examined their position and discovered with some horror that they had dug their hole in a bulging cornice clinging to the rock face right at the top of the Flatiron. It was the very place where in 1935 Sedlmayer and Mehringer, the first two ever to attempt to climb the Face, had died in a storm. There was nothing they could do to enlarge the hole because its walls were almost wafer-thin already – so thin that in the morning it was practically daylight inside the cave. To the left, the Third Icefield dropped down sharply; to the right was a steep snow slope that led eventually to the Second Icefield. The snow-hole was actually in the bottom of the cornice and if someone accidentally made a hole in the floor they could see all the way down to Grindelwald, nearly 5,000 feet below.

At 8.45 they made radio contact with Peter, apologising for missing the earlier time. 'We overslept,' said John – the understatement of the year. Peter gave them a fairly cheerful weather report: snow was forecast, but not too much, and with a good spell following. This put a summit push clearly on the cards.

Chris decided he had taken all the photographs he wanted to and packed his rucksack ready to leave. The other started to clear up the mess in the snow-hole and caught up on the brews they had missed the previous day.

By lunchtime the weather was still fine and the cave showed signs of having been organised. Chris had left for Scheidegg, making one less person to eat up the food. Peter Haag and Günther Strobel were climbing already. They had started up the crack system above their snow-hole. Layton and Dougal decided to climb in the afternoon so that they wouldn't get left behind.

The two teams were going to follow different lines again, but Layton, John and Dougal still hadn't decided which of two options to take. When they were studying their photographs of the Face it had seemed best to cross the Third Icefield to the Ramp, follow this for a pitch, and then cut back to an icy gully line leading to the top of a prominent pillar that finished about three rope-lengths below the Spider. Because of its position on the Face they christened it the Central Pillar. But there was another possibility: they could climb straight up the Third Icefield and try to get into the same gully line in its upper reaches.

Dougal traversed round from the snow-hole on to the Third Icefield and immediately decided to climb straight up. The ice was hard and fairly steep but he knew this route would go quickly; whereas he couldn't see all of the alternative line and what he could see looked difficult.

The Third Icefield went quickly: two long, calf-straining pitches, with the main difficulty the lack of protection. Dougal's tubular ice-screws were freezing up on him and he had only two of the dagger-type with him. Layton joined him at the top of the icefield and then pushed through quickly up a steep pitch on mixed ground. This led to an arête just below the Central Pillar.

There they met Peter Haag and Günther Strobel, who had reached the top of their crack system a short while before. Peter was belaying Günther as he climbed a little way ahead. Dougal and Layton chatted with him for a time and then abseiled back down to the Death Bivouac, fixing ropes as they went. It was late and there was a stormy sunset but they were pleased with the day's work. They clattered round the corner in great crampon leaps, to find John cooking in a now well-organised snow-hole.

There was a happy chatter as they ate. Dougal and Layton told John their news, which was that Peter Haag had told them the Germans were going to try a crack system to the right of the Central Pillar. This looked straightforward at first, but higher up it led into an overhanging chimney completely blocked near its top by a bulge of snow. Dougal thought from his experience of winter climbing in Scotland that it looked highly dangerous. 'It looks really way out,' he told Layton. 'I wouldn't touch it.' But while Dougal had been examining the chimney Layton had noticed a traverse line at the foot of the Central Pillar that would take them into the good chimney line leading to its top. The traverse was undoubtedly difficult but Layton thought he could climb it, whereas Dougal doubted whether the chimney the Germans had chosen was even possible.

John accepted their opinions and they decided to attempt the traverse the next day. The three felt buoyant and elated. They knew their route, they thought it would go, and they felt poised for a summit push.

But it was all too easy. Already dark clouds were rolling in. Even before they had finished their meal it was snowing heavily. Once again the weather said no.

When they woke on the morning of Friday 11 March, they found it had snowed all night. The sky was overcast and it looked as though more snow would fall at any time. The weather forecast that Peter gave them at 7.45 confirmed this. They held a quick council of war. Climbing looked as though it was now out of the question for at least two days, so they decided that Layton should go down to Scheidegg to sit out the bad spell there. They would stick to the plan of waiting for good weather on the Face so that they could start climbing again as soon as possible.

Layton left soon afterwards, saying happily 'See you' as he pulled himself through the entrance. John and Dougal asked him to fix a tent-sack over the entrance from the outside, and this he did, nailing it in place with ice-pitons. So right from the start John and Dougal were effectively walled in. They heard Layton's footsteps and the whipping of the fixed ropes as he made his way over to the German snow-hole for a courtesy visit before setting off down the Face.

What John and Dougal were contemplating was nothing less than a siege. They were going to sit on the North Face of the Eiger, in winter, until the storm had spent itself. The one thing that made this possible was their snow-hole, which would protect them from everything the mountain and the weather could hurl at them. Outside they could already hear the increasing swishing of the wind; soon it began to buffet at the hole. The tent-sack that Layton had nailed to the outside was held up from the inside by a shovel. The entrance was rather larger than it need have been because of the appalling conditions in which it had been dug, and already spindrift was starting to spurt in round the tent-sack. The back of the snow-hole was the rock of the Eiger itself, scarred with grooves and crevices. Spindrift trickled into the cave down these as well.

Because of what John called the 'insidious nature' of spindrift it got literally everywhere. As they had found during the day they had spent in the snow-hole below the First Band, if left to lie where it settled it dampened whatever it touched. Consequently they spent a large part of that first day in the snow-hole fighting to block off all the places where spindrift could come in. They fastened the bivouac sack across the entrance as tightly as they could, and stuffed socks and gloves into the gaps between the rock at the back of the hole and the snow that formed the roof. They also spent much time brushing the spindrift off things that it settled on.

Lunchtime brought more problems. They found they had no funnel with them to refill their paraffin stove, and all their paraffin was in a gigantic yellow gallon-size plastic canister. Dougal had to take off his gloves, promptly freezing his fingers on the metal stove, to perform the operation. They found they had no Meta fuel and Dougal had to preheat the stove with a candle instead. He finally got it alight, set it down and put a snow-filled pot on top of it. Gradually the flame got weaker and weaker and in five minutes it had gone out. The cold had crept up through the base of the stove and stopped the paraffin from vaporising. There was nothing for it but to keep reheating the stove while it was actually alight to stop it from going out again.

Water is normally no problem on a mountain in winter – you just dollop lumps of snow into a pot and melt it. But in digging out their snow-hole they had used up all the available spare snow – the walls were thin enough as it was and it would put the whole structure at risk to take any more snow from them.

So they had to hack into the hard ice forming the floor of the constricted back part of the cave. Wielding an ice-axe in such a confined space with the other occupant squeezing himself out of the way turned out to be a highly skilled operation in itself.

To eat, they had the food they had been planning to use for the summit push. They had reckoned on four days to the top from the Death Bivouac and they had enough brewing supplies for a further three days as well. But as Chris had gone with them to the Death Bivouac he had eaten into their summit rations. They had with them dried meat, bacon, peanuts, dried apricots and dried bananas. To make brews they had the usual Calcitonic and Minivit. But at that stage they did not worry about the problem of food for the days ahead. The longest period that either of them had spent in a snow-hole before was the one day in the cave at the bottom of the First Band. 'If anyone had told us we were going to be there for more than a couple of days we'd have laughed,' said Dougal afterwards. If they had thought there was even a chance they would be there for any longer than that, they would have come down at once. Besides, it was out of the question to think they might be up there and not climbing for any length of time. They always looked forward to the next forecast in the hope that it would promise them good weather; and always there was enough optimism in it for them to believe that in the not too distant future climbing would be possible.

This was partly because, on the ground, Peter and Chris were subconsciously aware of a need to keep John's and Dougal's spirits up and their hopes alive, and they always presented the optimistic aspect of a weather forecast first, or emphasised the report from whichever office was most hopeful. Partly, though, it was the fault of the weather itself. A huge high-pressure system was centred off the south coast of Ireland whose drift eastwards encouraged the forecasters to believe that it would eventually bring good weather to Switzerland. But it fooled everyone and stayed right where it was. The effect that these optimistic reports had on John and Dougal was to cheer them up temporarily and then to plunge them back into despair when they realised that climbing was still out of the question.

Dougal had been afraid that his comparative inactivity would make it difficult for him to get to sleep at night. But on Friday night he found that he had used up so much mental and physical energy in the continual war against spindrift that he fell asleep quite quickly.

At 2.00 a.m. he was woken from a deep, deep sleep by John saying 'Christ, Dougal, we've got to get up.' Dougal forced his eyes open and saw that spindrift had come in through the entrance and was lying on his sleeping bag. There was no alternative but to drag himself upright and set to work to clear it away. It took an hour of half-dazed brushing in bitter cold before he could flop back and gratefully sink back into sleep. At 5.00 a.m. the same thing happened all over again.

'What are the survival problems involved up there?' Peter asked John by radio the next day. 'Staying alive,' said John, and that Saturday, 12 March, he and Dougal began to work out a routine for dealing with the problems of existence at –20 °C. Waking up was always an effort – it used to take Dougal a good hour to become aware of everything around him and all that needed to be done. He felt drugged, and had to force his body to perform the day's preliminary tasks. First, as always, they had to clear away the spindrift, which would take them anything up to an hour. Then Dougal would start the breakfast brew-up. They would allocate themselves a share of the bacon and dried meat which they would munch stolidly and wash down with Calcitonic.

Breakfast might take another hour. After that there was nothing pressing to do – always excepting the interminable process of clearing away spindrift – so they would sink back into their sleeping positions and perhaps doze. Or they would talk – and talk and talk and talk. Several topics of conversation were sheer wish-fulfilment – like the plans to climb in Tahiti. 'There's a thousand-foot pinnacle rising sheer up in the middle of the island like a great phallic symbol,' John told Dougal. They laid plans to climb in every part of the world, from Alaska to the Himalaya. They also talked about food – the traditional subject of conversation of prisoners everywhere. They talked about the steak tartare followed by the whole Châteaubriant each they were going to have when they got back to Scheidegg. 'Torture,' Dougal said.

Dougal found himself recounting to John a complete history of Britain. John had asked Dougal where his ancestors came from, and Dougal told him they were members of a Celtic tribe that overran Britain during the decline of the Roman Empire. From that point Dougal had to explain the whole of Britain's polyglot ancestry. They talked about why they climbed, about women, about philosophy, about life in general. But they never talked continuously – there were always long reflective pauses.

They had worked out such a compact self-sufficient routine for themselves that they began to resent the radio calls, intrusions from the outside world, for breaking into it – particularly when they had to cut short a time-consuming doze to meet the call. On the ground, however, Peter, unaware of this, believed that the more contact John and Dougal had with Scheidegg the better. He thought this would help lessen any feeling of isolation, and give him and Chris more opportunities to encourage John and Dougal in their siege. He often suggested extra call times which John, out of politeness, agreed to. Even with walkie-talkie radios communication wasn't perfect.

John and Dougal were in a world of their own. All they could hear from outside was the hissing of spindrift avalanches as they slid down the Third Icefield and the hammering of the wind. Sometimes there was a terrifying cracking sound as the whole cornice developed a split. This was annoying as well as frightening because each time it happened it brought a fresh cloud of spindrift into the hole. Dougal was occasionally aware that the whole cornice could peel away from the rock and tumble down the Face – as it undoubtedly would when spring came. But this thought was so impossible to dwell on that he always suppressed it quickly. A less hardened man might have had difficulty in doing so, particularly as John or Dougal still sometimes accidentally pushed an ice-axe through the floor, giving spectacular views of Grindelwald or Kleine Scheidegg, depending on where in the cave the hole was made.

On Saturday evening both John and Dougal were forced to do something they had been putting off as long as possible, and that was to defecate. Urinating was not a problem because for some reason the urine didn't smell, and they each had a small hole by their sleeping bags which they used. But defecating was more difficult: they wore so many layers of clothing, the space was cramped, and there was the question of hygiene. They chose a site near the entrance and found that an extra problem was that the excrement definitely did smell.

Apart from this, they were in general comfortable. They had spread a ground sheet on the floor and their sleeping bags lay on foam-rubber mattresses. The Germans, who did not have mattresses, began to suffer from rheumatism, but this did not affect Dougal and John. But their feet were cold for most of the day, getting warm only at night, or after a hot drink. Before going to sleep Dougal took slow-acting Ronicol anti-frostbite tablets, which ensured that his feet would stay warm for at least four hours. Another source of discomfort was that on each of the first three nights Dougal had a strange dream. He imagined that there was a third man in the snow-hole, and moved over to give him more room. Each night he woke up to find himself squeezed against the wall. Thinking how silly he must appear, he uncurled into the space he had left.

For the first two days of the storm the rest of the team at Scheidegg had been languishing in the hotel lounge and bar watching the snow driving past the windows. They had had several visitors. Two British equipment dealers, Frank Davies from Ambleside and Graham Tiso from Edinburgh, for whom Dougal acted as an adviser, stopped by on their way to a trade fair in Germany. Norman Dhyrenfurth, leader of the American expedition to Everest in 1964, called to give John and the team his best wishes. Even so, those at Scheidegg were afflicted by a strong feeling of lassitude. They could rarely see the Face and the major events of the day were the radio calls.

But on the radio call at 11.45 on Sunday morning, 13 March, John dropped a bombshell among them. He asked to speak to Layton: 'Layton, I am not feeling well. I have sickness, I have fever, and I think a respiratory cold. I'd like some medicine when you come up. Can you see if there's a doctor at Scheidegg, please?'

Peter and Chris went to ask in the hotel office if there were any doctors staying at the hotel. There were no less than five – a party of four women and one man from Paris. Just before lunchtime Peter and Chris tracked them down and explained what had happened. Could they very kindly come and speak to John on the radio? Yes, they could – they would be delighted to help.

At 1.45 all five came to Peter's room. 'We have five doctors for you,' Peter told John. He translated their questions. What was his pulse? His breathing? Did he have fever? Was he vomiting? How much was he urinating? John said his pulse was 88 (though in this he was mistaken), he had fever, and he was urinating a lot. The doctors went into a huddle and then delivered their verdict. 'He need not come down at once. But if there is no improvement by tomorrow morning he should come down then. Really he should come down now; the mountain is not a place to be if he is not well. But we understand about the climb and the competition. We can leave it until tomorrow to see.'

Ever since they had started their siege in the snow-hole John and Dougal had discussed whether they should go back down to Scheidegg. John's illness was a new factor to be considered. Soon there was to be another one. That morning they had eaten the last of their bacon, which meant there would be no more hot meals for them until someone came up with more supplies – or until they went back to Scheidegg. The only substantial food they had now was a small amount of *viande sechée* which would last them for about two more days.

They had two other factors to think about. Even if it stopped snowing, how long would they have to wait before the Face was in good enough condition to climb again? If they started too quickly snow would be plastered everywhere and the spindrift avalanches would be pouring down. Secondly, what were the Germans going to do? What would happen if John and Dougal came down while Peter Haag and his four colleagues managed to sit out the bad weather on the Face? At that time John believed that whoever got ahead above the Death Bivouac would be in a strong position. It seemed that there would be only one good bivouac site – on top of the Central Pillar – between where they were now and the summit. Whoever got to the top of the Central Pillar first would be able to choose the best position – if there was room for more than one party at all. It was also possible that there was going to be only one obvious line from the Spider to the summit. John, Dougal and Layton still intended to make their Alpine-style push when the good weather eventually came and they did not want the larger German team on the route in front of them.

These, then, were the problems facing the whole team. On Sunday's radio call John asked Don if he had any ideas. 'No,' said Don. But he did add helpfully: 'I'll let you know if I think of anything.' The whole of Sunday was spent discussing the position. At lunchtime the weather reports were allowing Layton to hope that he might return to the Face with fresh supplies and medicine for John the next day. That evening Chris came up with an extremely favourable forecast. 'The next two days: cloudy with a wee bit of snow, steadily improving; on the third day, fairly good; and after that there could be a settled spell of five to six days.'

John asked Layton what conditions on the Face looked like. 'Very poor,' Layton told him. 'I noticed in particular the yellow and red wall above the Ramp. It's the first time I've seen this part of the Face completely plastered white.' John was not feeling any better in himself that evening. 'How are you doing, Dad?' Layton asked him. 'We'll forget that question,' said John. 'There's no question but that I'm a sick man,' he told Scheidegg, adding: 'But I'm not that sick.' Chris asked him if he thought he should come down to recuperate. 'In the past when I hit a bed I just go completely under but when I'm in a difficult situation I seem to recover all the faster.' This certainly appeared to be true – he had made some amazing recoveries. In any case it was now too late for him to come down that evening. The only sensible thing to do was to wait until the following morning to see how he felt then.

The next problem that had to be considered was the competitive element of the climb. What were the Germans going to do? 'It's really rather a complex problem now,' John said, 'with the conditions on the mountain bad and both parties poised to converge on the same route, and with neither knowing what the other one is doing and therefore anxiety and an increased feeling of competition.

'About the only acceptable compromise for everyone is a co-ordinated ascent. This is very good, but the big problem is that we don't have this conception of a great group going to the summit. And we don't want to come up the third or fourth rope as though we were pulled up by the Germans, because we are of course capable of doing the climb ourselves.

'And the thing about the way the Germans are doing it, by keeping on plodding on, is that with the possibility of good weather we can just drop all our gear and make the summit in three bivouacs, if not faster.

'It would be very good to talk to the Germans. It is theoretically possible to go ahead and push for this new bivouac, which is only three rope-lengths above our fixed ropes and two to three rope-lengths above theirs. You can foresee this ludicrous situation where the two teams are forced, because of lack of communication, to run for this bivouac site and perhaps even lose the whole ascent. I don't know if you realise it, but the Germans would have lost the ascent already if it had not been for our fixed ropes because they had lost their equipment in the storm. So there are many, many reasons for co-ordination at this point. Otherwise it becomes – as I said before – ludicrous.'

Chris and John wondered whether they should ask the Germans for formal discussions about each other's intentions, and whether they should join up. John at first thought that Chris and Jörg Lehne should have 'a regular sit-down-and-talk-it-out conference', but then he became worried in case it appeared that he was asking to join the German team.

In the end Chris suggested leaving it until the next morning before deciding what to do. 'That would still give you time to come down if you felt that was advisable without in fact displaying your hand at all. No one knows you're at all sick or that there's any thought of you coming down.'

' That sounds fairly good to me,' said John, and there the matter was left.

At 8.45 on Monday morning, 14 March, the five doctors filed into Peter's room and Peter started relaying their questions to John. At once it was clear that John was feeling remarkably better. He had stopped coughing in the night, he was in far less pain, he was urinating less, and he didn't feel nearly so cold. His pulse was down from 108 (the true reading) to 75. 'I feel very good this morning. I feel like staying up and I feel like climbing.' After a short huddle the doctors delivered their verdict. 'He need not come down now. We should like to check him again at the next radio call.' One of the doctors added: '*Dites-lui qu'on l'admire beaucoup.*'

So John's powers of recovery had once again proved to be remarkable for had the doctors known his true pulse-rate they would certainly have insisted on his coming down. The people at Scheidegg had been conditioning themselves to accept that he was going to have to, possibly even give up the climb. Peter had been in the unusual situation of hoping for bad weather so that if John did come down he wouldn't miss any climbing. Now one of the problems seemed to have vanished, literally overnight.

But one of the remaining four had suddenly become very big. That morning John and Dougal had looked at their food supplies: two slices of dried meat each, which they would eat that day. The question of fresh supplies could no longer be pushed aside. After the doctors had gone John spoke to Chris. 'The problem of staying up is now one of supplies. We're down to four days of brewing and about one day more of meat with absolutely nothing else. There's going to be a diminishing strength return. I'm afraid we're going to have to work out some method of supply.'

There were several possibilities. The best was that Chris and Layton should go up to the Death Bivouac with fresh supplies the next day. Chris had already agreed with Jörg Lehne that members of both teams should return to the Face together, taking it in turns to break trail. The weather forecast was 'reasonable', Chris said. 'But if the weather isn't better we may have to think again.'

'We can exist up here for another week,' John told him, 'but we're going to be losing strength considerably.'

Chris tentatively put forward the idea that if the weather stayed bad John and Dougal should come down, to be replaced by himself and Layton as soon as the weather improved.

There was a pause while John and Dougal discussed this. John came back on: 'It certainly is a fact that we should maintain two people up here, because otherwise when the conditions become climbable we're going to lose a fair amount of time.'

In that case, Chris said, it was just a question of deciding how to restock the bivouac, and whether this would be possible the next day. 'According to the weather forecast it is.'

Despite the problems, John and Dougal were in good spirits. John was happy that his illness appeared to be on the wane. From his radio call at 11.45 that morning Dougal seemed cheerful enough. 'We are covered with a mixture of Scots–American excrement,' he announced happily.

Chris told him that he had never seen the Face looking so pretty – 'like a great big white Christmas tree,' he said.

'I hope it's snowing on your head tomorrow as you come up with loads of goodies,' Dougal told him.

Chris told the two in the bivouac that he and Don would definitely come up with more food the next day. They had decided that the situation warranted their using the Jungfrau railway. The slopes below the Face were very deep in snow and undoubtedly avalanche-prone. And as well as being dangerous, the journey across them would be extremely hard work. So he and Don planned to catch the 9.50 train from Scheidegg to the Eigerwand station and go out on to the Face through the window. It only remained for them to get permission to do so.

As they had agreed with Jörg Lehne to go to the foot of the Face together, this meant a new discussion with the Germans. Chris and Peter met Harri Frey and arranged a conference in the bar that afternoon. At the appointed hour the teams met, sitting round one of the tables. The Germans were represented by Harri Frey, Jörg Lehne, Karl Golikow and Toni Hiebeler. Peter and Chris were there for the British–American team.

Chris opened the proceedings. 'Jörg, we've been thinking. We're a little worried about the snow on the slopes below the Face. We think they might avalanche. We want to go out on to the Face through the Eigerwand station window. Do you want to come with us?'

'No,' said Jörg.

That being the end of the conference, the two sides chatted inconsequentially for a time and then Peter and Chris joined the rest of the circus in the lounge for an atypical afternoon tea with sticky cakes.

On the evening radio call they told John the news. Chris said that they would now stick to their original plan of going with the Germans to the Face. They would bivouac in the first ice-cave on Tuesday night and come on up to the Death Bivouac on Wednesday morning.

There was a pause. 'Well, Chris, that leaves us a day without food,' said John. Chris explained that he and Don would have to wait for some more Jumar clamps that were due to arrive by post the next morning. 'Perhaps a better idea would be to send Layton on ahead to make the push all the way,' John suggested, to the amusement of everyone except Layton. Peter had his own smile wiped out when Chris suggested that he helped Layton break trail.

Chris told John that he thought there was some food in the bivouac cave at the top of the Second Band. 'There's noodles, potato mixture and tomato purée, so if you thought it was worth getting out for some exercise and climbing wasn't practical, it might be worthwhile going and getting this stuff. At least it would make a filling meal, even if there wasn't much nutrition.'

'Thank you for the advice,' John said tolerantly. 'We'll have to evaluate that.'

So the plans were that Peter and Layton should go to the bottom of the Face early the next day, Tuesday. Layton would go right on up to the Death Bivouac and Chris and Don would follow later with the Germans.

That evening Peter ran into Fritz von Almen, the hotel owner, who gave his opinion of the climb. 'They must be crazy up there after four days,' he told Peter. 'It will be impossible to get to the foot of the Face for another four days. What is John doing? Does he still intend to go on?' Peter assured him that John did.

Several newspapers were beginning to get excited about the fact that seven men – John and Dougal, and the Germans Haag, Strobel, Hupfauer, Schnaidt and Votteler – had now spent four days in snow-holes on the Face without moving and presumably running low on food. The London *Evening News* ran a story on the Tuesday, 15 March, written by Associated Newspapers' ageing Geneva stringer, one Hugo Kuranda. He used the name Arthur Durman, and it was headlined 'London climber in rescue bid'. 'London climber Chris Bonington, Manchester man Don Whylliams [sic] and American Layton Kor are to start out today for the Eiger North Wall in a dangerous attempt to bring urgently needed relief to Scotsman Dougal Haston and American John Harlin.' Don was delighted when he read the report. 'I've always wanted to be in a rescue,' he said. 'And wouldn't it be good if they had been trapped and we'd reached them? We could have radioed back: "Aye, they are trapped, and that makes ten of us!"'

The next day Kuranda had a similar piece in the London *Daily Sketch*, headlined: 'It started as a race ... now it's a rescue.'

> *'It began as a light-hearted race, almost in the mood of a boyish es-capade [he wrote]. But there was no laughter on the Eiger today and no dancing in the valley below, where the wives and sweethearts of the climbers wait. For sheltered in a tiny snow-hole, 11,200 feet up the wall, Dougal Haston (24) from Edinburgh, and John Harlin, a 30-year-old American, have sent a walkie-talkie message to their three comrades: "It is terribly grim up here. Can't you help us?" They have been marooned on the mountain since digging in last Thursday.*

> 'This afternoon Britain's Chris Bonington and the German leader Joerg Lehne led a combined rescue party up the Eiger.
>
> 'They ignored the warnings of the Swiss professional guides: "Don't go yet. There are avalanches waiting to kill you.
>
> '"Even the vibrations caused by your climbing boots may release some of them."
>
> 'The happy hours seem so far away, when Marilyn Harlin, pig-tailed Wendy Bonington, and Audrey Whillans would take turns at the big telescope on their hotel roof and tell each other what grand chaps their husbands were.
>
> 'Today the adventure has gone sour … '

'Why don't you get a hold of that guy and rope him down and straighten him out?' John asked Peter when he heard about the story. 'I'd like to kill the — —' was Dougal's reaction. Neither he nor John had ever sent the quoted radio message or anything like it. No Swiss guides ever gave such a warning to Chris. At any time during the five days they spent in the snow-hole John and Dougal could have come down the fixed ropes to Scheidegg. It was precisely to safeguard their retreat in a storm that they had left the ropes in place. The result of stories like this one was that the Munich *Bergwacht*, Bavaria's crack mountain rescue team, prepared to come to Scheidegg to help. Marilyn Harlin rang up anxiously to find out what was happening.

Meanwhile, back in the real world, John and Dougal continued their siege. On Tuesday morning, 15 March, Chris told John that the high-pressure system they had been expecting so long had moved only as far as Wales, but that it was still supposed to be coming. The plans for bringing up supplies had changed slightly: Layton was now going with Chris, Don and the Germans at 11.00 a.m. instead of setting off earlier with Peter. That way the load of trail-breaking would be evenly spread. Layton would continue right on up to the Death Bivouac by himself, climbing with a head-torch if necessary.

The party moved to Chris's room and the long narrow corridor outside it. Climbing equipment and the fresh supplies were spread out everywhere. Climbers sat on the floor threading bootlaces, doing up gaiters, sorting out personal gear. Don put on his clothes for going to the Face: a woollen vest and a duvet jacket. There was general happiness: whistling, laughing, shouting. Even if it was only an aching slog through deep powder snow to the foot of the Face, at last, after four days of complete inactivity, something was happening.

But at 10.00 a.m. Jörg Lehne and Harri Frey appeared in the corridor. 'I don't think we can go,' Jörg told them. 'I think it is too dangerous.'

There was a brief discussion.

'We are still going,' Chris told Jörg, not adding that John and Dougal had run out of food.

'OK,' Jörg said, 'I come too.' He and Harri disappeared.

There now ensued a phase of total indecision and prevarication. At first Layton and Jörg were to ski to the Face together at 11.00, followed later by everyone else. Then they were all to go to the Face together at midday, and perhaps bivouac in the ice-cave at the foot of the First Band. Gradually it became clear that no one wanted to spend that night on the Face. The plan that emerged from the quasi-rational discussion that continued all morning was that, in view of the thick snow below the Face, and the heavy loads, it would, by and large, on the whole, all things considered, be the safest and most practical thing if they broke trail on skis to the Face that afternoon, spent the night in Scheidegg, and returned to the Face the next morning. The decision having been reached, the whistling, laughing and shouting started up again.

Since everyone was going on skis this let Peter out, as his ability to ski was highly limited. He was, however, faced with the task of telling John and Dougal that they were not going to get any food that day. The party of five left Scheidegg at about 3.00 p.m. At 3.45 Peter made the radio call to John. Trying to make it appear that the plan that had evolved was the result of a balanced, logical discussion, Peter put on his best press spokesman's voice. 'Just after lunch Chris, Don, Layton, Jörg Lehne and Karl Golikow went up to the top of the Salzegg ski-run and are now making a traverse from there to the bottom of the fixed ropes. Their intention was to make a trail for tomorrow – that's if they're going by skis tomorrow – and also to do some of the load-carrying already so they'll be able to pick it up at the bottom of the fixed ropes tomorrow.'

To Peter's surprise, John didn't appear too upset at this change of plan; he was far more interested when Peter said that it was snowing at Scheidegg. 'How about a weather report, Pete? It's pretty important.'

The crucial news was that the high-pressure system appeared to have stopped and that there was no chance of its reaching Switzerland for at least thirty-six hours. 'Things don't look too good, Pete,' John said.

'I'd say they don't,' Peter answered. 'Have you considered coming down?'

'We're considering it very strongly now,' John told him, 'because of your weather report. I wish we'd had it two hours ago – we'd be down by now. We simply cannot come down until tomorrow, anyway. It will hang on your next two or three weather reports. If of course the weather reports are bad, I'm not altogether sure it's a good idea for the boys to come up.'

So things were gradually moving towards a decision to come down – to vacate the snow-hole and wait until the long-promised good weather actually came before sending anyone back to the Face. That evening Chris, Don and Layton came back from the foot of the Face and reported that snow conditions had been 'desperate'. Jörg Lehne and Karl Golikow had, however, set off up the fixed ropes carrying loads. Already as they started the first prusik it was snowing and beginning to get dark, but they said they would be back that evening.

The weather forecast was still bleak for the evening's radio call. The famous high-pressure system was stationary and was not expected to move in and push away the snowy weather for several days.

'It would seem to me that the best thing would be to retreat until the weather turns good,' said John. What clinched the decision was the very bad condition the Face appeared to be in: once it stopped snowing, it would be one or even two days before climbing could start again, and in that time two of them could push back up from Scheidegg to the high point. Secondly, there was the problem of diminishing strength, particularly now that John and Dougal had still not been reached with fresh supplies. 'I think both teams are getting to the stage where the longer they stay up, the weaker they're going to become,' said Chris. 'I think you're going to be very pushed to take full advantage of the good weather by staying up there. I think the team that's fittest and strongest is the team that's going to be successful.' John had, after all, been ill, and was still not fully recovered; it would be best for him to have some rest in the comfort of Scheidegg. A little reluctantly, still thinking that fresh supplies could be brought up the next day, John agreed.

At 8.30 Karl and Jörg had still not returned and Chris and Peter were beginning to feel anxious about them. There was no doubt that the slopes below the Face were avalanche-prone. But there was nothing they could possibly do until first light. However, at 9.00 Karl and Jörg, iced-up and covered with snow, came striding up the railway track and disappeared without saying a word towards the Stöckle hut.

That night in the bar Fritz von Almen told Peter: 'Those men who went to the Face today were lucky, they had the hundred-to-one chance. Hilti von Allmen was not so lucky; he was killed by an avalanche while skiing yesterday.'

On the morning of Wednesday 16 March cloud still hid the Face and it was snowing at Scheidegg. The high-pressure system was still moving painfully slowly, and in addition John revealed that his illness appeared to have 'gone into a certain amount of bronchitis'. To encourage John to come down, Chris offered to go back up with Layton if the weather improved before John was ready to return. John said they would stick to their plan and come down. 'Cheers, mate, see you,' Chris said.

Up in the snow-hole Dougal cleared away five days' excrement from the entrance and thrust the shovel through the hole. He wriggled out, clipped on to the fixed line, and stood up. A weird unbalanced feeling crept over him, and it was five minutes before he could start moving. It was really cold. The wind was whipping flurries of spindrift into their faces. It took the whole of the unpleasant traverse to Peter Haag's snow-hole before their circulation got going properly. It was strange to start moving again.

They stopped and spoke to Peter Haag and Günther Strobel. The Germans didn't look too happy, Dougal thought, but were determined to stick it out. He and John thought they were wrong. As they set off down the ropes leading to the Second Icefield, they felt slightly lightheaded through lack of food.

So they were coming down at last. Peter and Chris prepared to go and meet them. Chris set off on his skis at 10.00 and Peter caught a train to Alpiglen half an hour later.

When he got off the train he was afraid he might have missed John and Dougal, so he asked a railwayman clearing snow off the line if he had seen two climbers. 'Yes,' said the railwayman, handing Peter a pair of binoculars. 'There they are.' He pointed high up on the Face. John and Dougal were still on the fixed ropes above the Second Band. Higher still, on the Second Icefield, were two of the German team, who turned out to be Sigi Hupfauer and Günter Schnaidt.

Peter reckoned he had a good two hours to wait, so he walked off up the track to look for Chris. In a quarter of an hour he arrived at a railway tunnel. At the other end, about 400 yards away, he saw Chris on skis in the snow. 'Chris, come down here,' he yelled.

'No, you come up here,' Chris shouted back.

'How?'

'Along the top of the tunnel.'

A steep bank of snow led up above the tunnel. Peter placed his foot as high up it as possible and tried to stand up. He sank to his waist in snow and decided to retreat.

'Chris, you come down the tunnel roof.'

Chris set off cautiously on skis. After about 50 yards he stopped. 'I'm going back. It's too f—g steep.' He turned round and skied back to the beginning of the tunnel. He and Peter looked at each other.

'Why don't you come through the tunnel?' Chris yelled.

'Because of the trains, Chris,' Peter yelled back.

'I don't suppose there are any coming,' Chris shouted hopefully.

Peter stopped thinking about the problem and set off into the tunnel. In five minutes he was through and in another ten he had got his breath back.

It was now a glorious morning. The clouds were clearing rapidly but it was bitterly cold. They stood on top of the tunnel watching the tiny red figures creeping down the Face. But after ten minutes they were both shivering, so they went and sat in a cave leading off the railway tunnel. Every now and then they went out to see how far John and Dougal had got. Finally Chris suggested: 'Let's go and meet them.' Peter had dressed to meet John and Dougal at Alpiglen station, but he did have gloves and gaiters, so he agreed and set off into the thigh-deep snow.

High above them Dougal was in trouble. The abseiling had gone without incident until the 300-foot rope down from the top of the First Band. He was about half-way down it when he noticed that the rope was beginning to get very tight. At first he thought that someone had tied it off to an expansion bolt. He carried on happily towards the place where he thought it had been fixed, when there was a sudden violent thrust and he was catapulted 30 feet against an overhang. The collision completely winded him and he very nearly let go of the rope. What had happened was that the rope had been blown sideways and had caught round an overhang. When he had nearly reached this point his weight had freed the rope. Dougal held on tight as he slid the remaining distance down the rope and collapsed in the snow at the foot of the Band. But he recovered quickly, and together he and John started down the last 2,000 feet of fixed ropes. In half an hour they were at the bottom of the Face.

Peter and Chris now realised they had forgotten to bring anything to drink or eat – not even a bar of chocolate. Then John slid away from the foot of the Face and came swooping down the slope on his skis which had been left in the cave at the foot. About 200 feet lower down there was a flurry of snow as he took a big fall. Dougal now appeared, sat down in the snow, and started a monster glissade. Snow piled up around him and in front of him as he overtook John.

Peter and Chris stood on a small ridge, just in the sun. Soon the two parties could shout to each other, with great exuberant yells. Dougal came ploughing towards them. 'Hi, man!' he shouted. John scythed up on his skis and stopped in a spray of snow. 'What are you doing here, Pete?'

'We came to meet you, John.'

Peter, with an 8-millimetre camera, and Chris, taking stills, floundered around John and Dougal. Then the four stood together, panting and laughing. John had a long black streak down his cheek. 'The stove blew up,' he said, and laughed again and then coughed badly, spitting into the snow. 'It's great to be back. It was really cold up there this morning.'

They were joined by Sigi Hupfauer and Günter Schnaidt, who had shared a pair of skis between them and were now covered in snow. All six set off back to Alpiglen, Peter and Dougal walking, the others skiing. At the tunnel entrance Dougal sat in the snow to take off his crampons. A train passed and the passengers stared out through patches in the misted-up windows, perhaps amazed to see two men sitting in the snow with wide grins on their faces.

They set off down the tunnel, and were half-way through when they heard the clatter of a train on the line. They saw its headlamps as it entered the tunnel and they ran up the line towards it and just in time dived into an opening in the tunnel wall. 'Climbers Killed in Tunnel Horror,' Peter thought to himself. The six met up again at Alpiglen station and stood together and talked. The weather was now perfect. To the east and north the last traces of cloud were disappearing. It was still very cold but beautifully keen and clear. Their train arrived and they packed into it. The sun was just coming over the West Ridge and as they passed they squinted up at the Face, towering impassively above them.

# Chapter VI

17 March was the second perfect day running and Chris and Layton decided to carry out their plan of returning to the Face. Chris said he thought he would stay up for three or four days, until John and Dougal came back. When that would be depended largely on how ill John was; he was going to have a check-up at Interlaken hospital that afternoon. Chris would have to come down when he and Dougal returned to the Face: there wasn't room for four people in the bivouac on top of the Flatiron.

Chris and Layton, each carrying 40 pounds of food and fresh supplies, left Scheidegg at 8.00 that morning, together with three of the German team: Jörg Lehne, Karl Golikow and Rolf Rosenzopf. From Salzegg to the foot of the Face there was some of the track left made by the trek with fresh supplies two days earlier, although in places it had been avalanched away. All five reached the foot of the First Band by midday. The Germans prusiked up the First Band first and it was about two hours before the last of the three was safely up. In the meantime Chris and Layton sat in their snow-hole at the foot of the First Band brewing tea. When they could eventually continue climbing it took them another two and a half hours to arrive at the Death Bivouac, which they reached at 6.00 p.m. During the prusiking Chris noticed that the fixed ropes were showing signs of wear, particularly where they ran over projections of rock.

During the day the weather became quite perfect and Peter Haag and Günther Strobel started climbing again, after a lay-off of six days. In the evening Layton went across to their bivouac to ask how they had got on. 'They're at the top of the Pillar,' he told Chris when he came back. The news meant that the Germans had reached what was thought to be the last good place for digging a snow-hole before the summit, and would once again get the best position – if indeed there was room for more than one snow-hole at all. And the old anxiety about having to wait behind while the Germans made the route ahead returned. 'We were a bit depressed,' Chris said afterwards.

In Scheidegg later that evening Peter met Mick Burke, another British climber, and told him that Chris had said the Germans had reached the top of the Pillar. 'But that's not possible,' said Mick. He had been watching the Germans until late that afternoon and they were still below a huge plug of snow that filled the top of the chimney. But there was nothing they could do to tell Chris.

That morning Peter and John had gone down to Lauterbrunnen for the funeral of Hilti von Allmen. It was the first time Peter had left Kleine Scheidegg for eighteen days, and it turned out to be the only time he was to do so during the whole climb. He had met Hilti when he was in Switzerland with photographer John Cleare in November. 'Everybody's thinking about the direttissima,' Hilti had said. 'It will be done.' John knew Hilti well.

Martin Epp, the Swiss guide from Wengernalp, was one of the pall-bearers. 'I just can't believe it's happened,' he had told Peter two days earlier. Most of the village followed the coffin from the house where Hilti had lived with his parents to Lauterbrunnen's graveyard.

John had arranged to take the train to Interlaken to go to the hospital for a check-up after his illness. The French doctors at Kleine Scheidegg had said he should do this before they prescribed anything for him. He and Peter waited for half an hour in the restaurant opposite Lauterbrunnen station. Peter asked John if he had lost many climbing partners. 'I've lost three in the last year, including the one who would have been with me on this climb now – Erich Friedli.'

What did John think of the dangers of climbing? 'I reason it this way: your family accept you and have accepted you for what you are, and they wouldn't want you to change, which you would be doing if you gave up climbing. Climbing is dangerous, and there's no getting away from it, people do get killed. But death's just a part of it all.'

John caught the train down to Interlaken shortly before 1.00 p.m., hoping to make it back up to Kleine Scheidegg that night. Peter caught the train up to Scheidegg.

Every Thursday the hotel at Scheidegg held a cold buffet dinner – in effect, as much as you could eat for 20 francs. Staying at the hotel at the time was a German businessman, Horst Schramm, whose daughter attended the American School at Leysin where Marilyn Harlin taught. 'John's a very good friend of mine,' he told people, and on the strength of it generously asked the members of the team down at Scheidegg to be his guests at the buffet dinner. Dougal, Wendy Bonington, Don Whillans and Peter came – and of the four only Peter wore a tie, the other three arriving in brightly coloured pullovers. 'I wouldn't have come if I'd known it was going to be like this,' said a subdued Don, looking at the dinner jackets and evening dresses all around him. Still, the food was good, despite the dignified scramble for the pieces of lobster that were going. After three good helpings of cold meat and fish, Dougal finished up with two gigantic pieces of chocolate cake. ''S guid,' he said to Peter between mouthfuls. Just before midnight the four excused themselves and moved into the bar.

At 12.30 a.m. Peter left the lounge, where he had been chatting up the *Sunday Times*, to go back to the bar. In the hotel lobby he met Horst Schramm, red-faced, looking around at people and moving excitedly from one foot to the other. He grabbed Peter: 'Do you know what some son of a bitch has just said to me? Some man in the dinner came up to me and complained to me because the climbers were wearing pullovers. It's up to me who I invite to dinner. And do you know what sort of man he is? He makes hairpins. Hairpins. I shall protest to the management.' Peter told the others what had happened. Don's face hardened. After sitting for some time saying nothing he got up and went out. The others sat in nervous silence. After ten minutes Don came back. 'Couldn't find t'booggers,' he announced. They all sat back in their chairs and relaxed.

Chris and Layton got up early on Friday, 18 March, to make what would be the first climbing progress by the team for a week. They made radio contact with Scheidegg at 7.45. Peter gave Chris the weather forecast – fine but unsettled – and then told him that Mick had been watching the Germans the previous day: 'They definitely did not reach the top of the Pillar.' This news encouraged Chris and Layton to climb even more. They looked out of the snow-hole and saw a sky covered with light grey cloud. They decided it was high enough not to mean bad weather, so they got dressed and left the snow-hole to climb to the previous high point.

Layton went up the fixed ropes first. But in the short time it took him to reach the foot of the Central Pillar, the weather had changed. The wind had started blowing and spindrift avalanches were coming down. Chris, shouting hard to make his voice carry against the wind, called to Layton: 'It's no bloody good, how about coming back?' Layton agreed. By lunchtime they were back in the snow-hole. The German team did not try to climb that day either.

John came back from the hospital at Interlaken that morning – he hadn't got away in time to catch the last train up the previous night. The morning's edition of *Blick* had said that John had been admitted to hospital with pneumonia and that he would hardly be able to take part in the climb any more. Reuter's had rung Peter from Geneva to ask if this was true 'before giving it out'. 'It's bronchitis,' John said when he saw Peter. 'But they say I'm getting over it now.'

'We're prepared for a long siege, man,' Chris told John when the two made radio contact at 1.45. 'There's no question of climbing in these conditions. We'll just have to sit out the bad weather.' But John was very optimistic. 'It seems as though we have a major winter change at the present time.' He explained that the cold air masses that normally influenced winter weather had finally broken through from Scandinavia. Later that day he forecast 'five, or ten, or even fifteen days' of settled weather. Dougal asked Chris if the bivouac was all right. 'It's bloody fabulous – really comfortable,' Chris told him. Their one problem was that they had only enough fuel for two or three days. John had lent some to the Germans and Chris had gone over to ask them about it. 'Trouble is, they don't seem very keen to give any of ours back.' Chris suggested that Dougal should try to make it up to the Death Bivouac with more fuel before they ran out. 'We'll review the situation when we get more weather reports,' said Dougal, unmoved. Chris reported that Peter Haag was still looking very fit after his twenty-three days on the Face. 'I prefer to stay up here,' Peter Haag had said. 'It's more peaceful.'

Chris spent the afternoon reading *Modesty Blaise*. Layton occasionally slept. Outside they could hear the muffled roar of the wind and the swish of the powder-snow avalanches as they swept down the Third Icefield. Just as Dougal and John had found during the early part of their five-day wait in the snow-hole, they too had the problem of spindrift leaking in at the entrance, even though they had covered it with a spare sleeping bag. ('So that's where my sleeping bag went,' muttered Peter.) Everything near the entrance was quickly covered with a thin layer of fresh snow. During the afternoon John wondered what it would be best for Chris and Layton to do. There was a good chance that the weather would turn good and stay that way, he thought. But he didn't want Chris and Layton to sit in the snow-hole doing nothing for four or five days as he and Dougal had done. It might be better for them to come down and wait for the good weather at Scheidegg. He talked about the problem with them during the evening.

'I think it would be best to come down if the weather's going to be bad,' said Layton. 'What are the Germans planning to do?'

'We couldn't care less at this moment, Layton,' John replied. 'I really think the best thing is that we stay fresh. With the fixed ropes we can be back up before the conditions become possible to climb. That way everyone stays strong.'

Chris agreed that it was essential not to miss another day's climbing, but thought that if there were only going to be a couple of days of bad weather it would be best to stay up. The three decided to wait until the next morning's weather forecast. If it were good, they would stay up; if not, they would come down and wait for good weather at Kleine Scheidegg.

Saturday dawned cold and crisp, with just a trace of high cirrus in the sky. John phoned for the weather forecasts and spoke to Chris and Layton at 7.45. 'The weather report confirms what I gave you last night, except of course that we have what seems to be beautiful weather,' he told them. Because of his Air Force training, John always placed emphasis on weather forecasts. Don Whillans, on the other hand, always went by what he could see. 'The only time weather forecasts are right is when they say it's going to be bad,' Don explained. John seemed to be suggesting that Chris and Layton should come down and wait at Scheidegg for the long clear spell definitely forecast for Monday. 'There's no question that when the high pressure is in dominance we will have five-plus to ten or even fifteen days' good weather,' he told them.

Layton and Chris were reluctant to come down. 'While we have this good weather it might be worth our while trying to get out and do some work on the Face,' said Chris. 'If you can actually do some constructive work, then I agree,' John told him.

Chris said he and Layton would get out to the Face and see what it was like.

They left the snow-hole and went up the fixed ropes to the foot of the Central Pillar. Through the telescopes at Scheidegg the Central Pillar looks very steep and very smooth. Close to, it looks exactly the same. When Chris and Layton arrived at its foot Jörg Lehne and Karl Golikow were already tackling a chimney going up to the top of the Central Pillar to its right. They had come to a halt eight days earlier below a huge overhanging cornice of snow. 'I'm not sure how they're going to get round it,' said Chris during the morning's second radio call.

He and Layton planned to open up the route to the top of the Pillar by traversing leftwards across its base. The pitch was very definitely Layton's lead. Here, as on the First Band, his ten years' experience of American rock climbing proved their worth. The rock was smooth and almost vertical, with snow clinging to it in places. Instead of his beloved delicate Kletterschuhe, he was wearing a pair of heavy-soled double-boots. Despite the cold, he climbed with bare hands. He leant far to his left, placed a piton, banged it in and hung an étrier from it. He would move to this and repeat the process. The rock was poor, brittle and compact, and twice the pitons he had placed came out in his hand as he prepared to hang an étrier from them. The exposure was immense – above, the 300-foot Pillar; below, 3,000 feet of space. The traverse took three hours.

Chris made a radio call just as Layton disappeared around the corner towards a belay stance. 'The thought of following Layton terrifies me,' he said. Following Layton on artificial pitches was amusing for everyone except the person actually having to do it. Several times on the traverse Chris moved to an étrier on one peg, only to find he could not reach back to take out the peg he had just left. They had to stay there.

Layton's traverse finished round the corner, and the stance was at the foot of an ice gully. As they had hoped and expected, the gully led directly to the top of the Central Pillar nearly 300 feet above them. The gully was steep and the ice looked thin in places but the route would definitely go – as opposed to the line taken by the Germans, about which there could be no such certainty.

Layton had climbed in Alaska, but the bulk of his experience was of climbing in scorching heat in California and Colorado. The tradition of American rock climbing is to give oneself more protection than British climbers would. Layton used the same technique on the ice-pitch he now started to lead. Chris watched as Layton put in three ice-screws in the first ten feet and decided he was prepared to lead the pitch without protection – for one thing, this would save time.

The ice was thin, in places only an inch thick, and Chris placed only two shaky-looking ice-pegs in the whole run-out. Layton thought it looked very dangerous. The pitch took Chris one and a half hours, and when he reached a stance the top of the Central Pillar was only one more pitch above him. But it was already getting dark, so he abseiled back down to Layton at the foot of the Central Pillar, very pleased with the day's progress.

The two were now faced with having to make the diagonal abseil on the rope that they had fixed at the foot of the Central Pillar. Layton went first and got across without too much difficulty. Chris had been much impressed with the American technique of abseiling by passing the rope through a karabiner,[1] which then acts as a friction brake. The 3,000-foot drop below the diagonal traverse impressed him so much that he decided to use two karabiners instead of one. He clipped into the rope and set off. The rope ran smoothly enough to start with. But as he went on he slowed down, and exactly at the half-way point where the rope started to rise again towards the other side of the Pillar, he came to a halt.

He was there for an hour. The rope with his weight on it was so tight that he could not get any slack in it to unclip one of the karabiners. If he pulled on one side of it, it tightened the other side even more. Layton, sitting securely in the gathering darkness on the other side of the traverse, encouraged him: 'It's going to be a cold bivouac tonight, Chris.' Finally Chris freed himself by the rather desperate expedient of undoing his karabiner brake completely – though he did first attach himself to the rope with another karabiner. Next time they made the traverse they roped up first.

On the way back to the snow-hole they met Jörg Lehne. 'How did you get on?' asked Chris. 'It's a dead end,' said Jörg. He and Karl Golikow had spent the morning in their chimney and had finally decided that it would not be safe to try to pass the snow overhang that blocked their way. Jörg asked Chris and Layton if they would drop a rope to him when they reached the top of the Central Pillar. They readily agreed.

Events on the mountain had been hidden from the watchers at Kleine Scheidegg all day. At 6.45 Peter made the usual radio call to the Face, but there was no contact – Chris was still trying to free himself from his American double karabiner brake. At 7.45 Peter tried again. His radio crackled alive and Chris came on. 'Things have gone very well,' he reported. 'We're only 100 feet below the top of the Pillar and it's absolutely straightforward climbing ahead. We missed the call at 6.45 because I had this epic terrifying descent.' Peter told him that they had seen nothing all day. Chris said they had been above the cloud. There had been a few spindrift avalanches, but apart from that it had been 'fabulous but very cold'. Chris then reported on the day's climbing by the

---

1 Karabiner – a snap-link with a spring-loaded gate; used for belays and runners.

Germans. 'They're completely stuck. They just went up into their chimney and came down very early this morning.' He told how Jörg had asked if they would drop him a rope. Both Chris and Layton said they had really enjoyed themselves.

People were happy that evening in Kleine Scheidegg too. Dougal was pleased that the decision about the route he and Layton had made six days before on the Third Icefield had paid off. John felt that the team's careful study of the Face was now proving its worth. 'It's the turning-point of the climb,' he said in the Gaststube that night.

'We've made rather a radical decision,' Chris said with some diffidence at the start of the 11.45 radio call the next day. 'Though it is a temporary one until you actually ratify it. Layton and Charlie Golikow are climbing together up the Pillar. This seems quite a good compromise to me as it's inevitable that we're going to be following the same route. What do you think of this?'

'Well, it's a lot to swallow at the moment, Chris,' said John. 'I'll have to think about it. Off-hand it sounds good except I think it should have come a hair later, after we had already reached the top of the Pillar. How did this decision come about?'

It stemmed from the impasse the Germans had reached in their route the previous day. Jörg Lehne had come across to the British–American snow-hole that morning and said that he thought it would be sensible to climb together and not have two parallel lines. 'It's we who are asking you whether we can join you. We're not stuck completely. If you don't agree we can go to the right or just follow you up. But it doesn't seem sensible to climb on separate routes a few metres apart,' Jörg had said. One advantage that Chris could see in joining forces with the German team was that there would now be far more pitons and fixed ropes available to both teams. An additional motivation – which Chris revealed later, with characteristic frankness – was that if Layton climbed with Karl Golikow, he would be free to take photographs.

John was worried about the amalgamation for several reasons. As he had explained to Chris, he thought it had come just one day too early. Although he believed that climbing had great potential value in fostering internationalism, he was tired of being misrepresented in the Press – he had had a particularly bad deal from several Swiss newspapers in the waiting period before the climb, when he had tried to maintain some degree of secrecy. 'I don't want it to come out in the Press that we were taken up the mountain,' he told Chris. He wanted to make the gesture of friendship, but he wanted there to be no possibility of its appearing that he was asking for help. If Chris and Layton had climbed to the top of the Central Pillar – which they had almost reached the previous day – and then agreed to an amalgamation, there could have been no risk of this happening.

There was another point worrying John. He was still hoping to make an Alpine-style assault on the summit just as soon as the weather permitted. There was a chance that he would be able to do this from at least the Spider, perhaps even from the top of the Central Pillar, 300 feet below. Leaving aside the question of the purity or otherwise of the two methods, Alpine and Himalayan, he still thought that a quick thrust for the summit offered the best chance of success, particularly as there was the continued risk of a sudden spell of bad weather. 'I don't want us to be committed to climb with the complete German team. This is just too big and it isn't in our scheme of things,' he told Layton later that day. 'Now if they want to join up with us, say just Lehne and Charlie, to go with us to the summit, then that's fine.' John was not against the teams joining up in principle; but he did not want Layton or Chris to commit their team to a full-scale amalgamation before he had the chance to think the matter out.

Before lunch Don Whillans said goodbye to everyone down at Scheidegg. He had taken three weeks off from his job as sports instructor and moral tutor at the Leysin American School and the school could spare him no longer. He was to be replaced by Mick Burke, an Englishman who also taught sports at the school. Aged twenty-five, from Wigan, Mick was a very good climber who in 1965 had made the second ascent of the Hemming–Robbins direct start to the Magnone route on the west face of the Dru. The route had not been repeated since it was first put up in 1962, and it involved a number of pitches of VI and VI+, the hardest gradings there are. Mick had also climbed the Walker Pillar on the Grandes Jorasses and the Bonatti Pillar on the Dru. He and Chris made as superb a climbing team as had Chris and Don.

At lunch in the Gaststube John asked Peter to try to meet as many of the journalists as possible to explain why Layton and Chris were climbing with the Germans. Harri Frey habitually gave out news about the German team in press releases over the tapes and John didn't want there to be any misinterpretation of what had happened. Peter rang up Guido Tonella in Geneva, and told the two German television teams and any other journalists he saw, including Harri Frey himself.

After lunch John spoke to Chris again on the radio. Chris was making a brew with Jörg Lehne and John asked Chris to tell him that he would discuss whether to make a coordinated attempt with him the next day. Chris said that Jörg had told him that the Germans were providing for two teams of four to go from the Spider to the summit – a faster one and a slower one. Chris thought a possible method of amalgamating would be to have three summit teams from the Spider. And Chris said that Jörg always accepted that the three members of John's team should be in the lead team. But John wouldn't be drawn. He said he would discuss it with Jörg when he met him the next day.

While the discussions were going on Layton was climbing with Karl Golikow, perhaps the most cheerful member of the German team. He would happily climb up the fixed ropes on the Second Icefield hand over hand; or move between the snow-holes at the Death Bivouac without clipping into the fixed ropes running between them. His favourite English expression was 'It's a hard life,' which he would repeat with a wide grin while being deluged with spindrift avalanches or wading through the snow at the foot of the Face. His easy-going nature was testified to by the fact that he had had 250 metres of falls in his climbing career.

He and Layton returned to the previous day's high point, one pitch below the top of the Central Pillar. There was a poor belay stance – a platform stamped out of the snow and ice. Layton belayed himself by placing a bolt and two pitons into the Central Pillar itself, just to his right. The pitch was a narrow gully and very steep – about 70 degrees. Karl climbed it by bridging on each wall. 'Charlie only got one peg in on the whole pitch, and that wasn't worth much,' said Layton. 'When he slid down a couple of feet I thought he was going to kill both of us.' The final moves were over rotten ice blocks. Karl reached the top of the Central Pillar and brought Layton up. The irony was that both teams had hoped to find a place for a snow-hole there but the snow appeared too thin and steep to dig one.

Between the top of the Central Pillar and the Spider were 300 feet of climbing on mostly vertical rock. Layton took over the lead. Thirty feet of rock and ice led to a vertical groove that disappeared into an overhang about 100 feet up. The climbing was artificial but the cracks were good and Layton was able to place pitons securely. At the overhang he could follow the corner formed where it met the Face and was not forced out so that he was hanging free. Layton arranged a sling belay about six feet above the overhang. It was late in the afternoon now, so he secured the rope and abseiled down to the top of the Central Pillar. Karl prusiked up the rope to take out the pitons and the two went back down to their snow-holes.

At 7.45 p.m. John spoke to Layton on the radio. Layton thought he was still 200 feet below the Spider and was delighted to hear that only 50 feet of climbing remained before they reached the ice gully that formed the Spider's right leg.[1]

A second piece of good news was the weather forecast. 'The weather report is a go, is a go,' said John. 'I want to organise things to the point of a complete departure for the summit.'

At last it seemed that the weather would hold long enough for a summit push. There were two choices: 'Our plan is either to bivouac at the Death Bivouac tomorrow night and then leave very early, or else take our bivouac

---

1 Only four of the Spider's eight legs are clearly visible on the Face.

gear up to the top of the Pillar and make a platform there.' Layton explained that he didn't think this second idea was possible, and suggested taking off for the summit from the Spider.

John and Layton talked about the possible joining up of the teams. Because he had now decided to go hard and fast for the summit, John was against a full-scale amalgamation. He wondered if two of the German team – say Jörg and Charlie – would like to go with them.

'That would be a good deal,' Layton said, 'but I'm sure they won't go for it. I think perhaps they want to get everyone to the summit, so that taking off by ourselves would be the only thing to do. It would be nice to join up but … I don't know.'

The important thing, though, was the decision to go for the summit. John told Layton to carry on to the Spider with Jörg and Karl the next day but to have his personal gear ready for John and Dougal to bring on up.

Layton said he would need more pitons – he had some Chromolly left but not enough. John promised to look for some. He and Dougal would leave at midnight. After three weeks continually on the Face the summit push was on.

# Chapter VII

So this was it. John and Dougal had already sorted their personal gear and the food for the summit push. They looked for the things that Layton had asked for and then went to bed to try to get some sleep before departing at midnight on 20 March. But it was impossible; as usual before leaving for an important climb, thoughts whirled around in Dougal's mind. But he was grateful for the rest. He was in Peter's room, which meant that Peter had to wait downstairs in the bar. At midnight John decided that they didn't need to leave until 1.00 a.m., but at 12.30 Peter got fed up with drinking by himself and went back to his room. They talked quietly as Dougal got ready. 'Good luck,' said Peter as Dougal left. 'See you at the summit.'

The head waiter, a Sicilian called Mario who was very friendly with the climbers, had arranged breakfast for John and Dougal in a small room opposite the bar. They felt strange in their full Eiger winter outfit as they crept past the drinkers in the bar. It seemed as though they belonged to another world – and very soon they would. They slowly munched their huge steaks, wondering when they would see another. There were whispered goodbyes and they went out into the frozen night. They exchanged few words. They knew the snow slopes below the Face so well that they could almost have climbed them in their sleep.

They reached the beginning of the fixed ropes in good time, and continued their robot procession to a point about half-way up the easier first third of the Face. Dougal was climbing ahead up the ice by himself when he found that the climbing was becoming quite difficult. Then he remembered the pitch from their very first attempt on the climb. Surely there should be a fixed rope on it? John arrived and agreed with him. They looked around and saw the missing rope hanging 50 feet to the right. It had been blown across by the wind, and was quite out of reach. They muttered dark oaths about Chris, who must have abseiled down the rope the night before. There was nothing for it but to solo up to the next section of fixed rope. This jerked them forcibly out of their state of reverie; pitches of unroped ice-climbing at 5.00 in the morning would disturb most dreams, Dougal thought. But they got up safely and were soon sitting brewing up in the first ice-cave. They made the most of the rest; this was where the hard work would start, long wild sections of prusiking with heavy packs. John's bronchitis was beginning to trouble him again: Dougal had been feeling for him as coughs racked him on the fixed ropes below.

They took the last of the food from the cave and loaded up. The long overhanging prusik up the First Band always took at least half an hour and Dougal left the cave first, leaving John brewing up. He tried keeping his pack on his back but as soon as he put his weight on the prusik loops he was whipped over backwards. He came down again and fastened his pack to a trailing sling instead. After that everything was as normal as it could be for someone swinging free on Jumar clamps over a drop of 2,000 feet. Progress was tedious, even though Dougal's life literally hung on the 7-millimetre rope up which he was mechanically sliding his clamps. It was the exact converse of real climbing: even though he was in control of his own mind and emotions, Dougal was not in control of the whole situation. His life depended not on himself and his decisions but on the strength of the rope and its anchorage.

As Dougal reached the top of the Second Icefield he saw Layton nearly 1,000 feet above him, gently swinging in his sling belay, just below the Spider. Dougal shouted up: 'How's it going, big Daddy?' 'Just great, man' – Layton's reply, loud and clear, floated down through the wisps of cloud above. Lifted up by Layton's mood, Dougal moved on up the Flatiron and just before midday arrived at the Death Bivouac. He started brewing happily. Some time later John arrived, still troubled by coughing. He joined Dougal and together they gratefully downed hot drinks.

The weather was superb. When they went out of the snow-hole they could see Layton high above them. Jörg Lehne had led a long mixed pitch, some artificial, some free, to a stance just below the Spider. Layton had climbed up the ice gully that formed the Spider's right leg and was now leading into the actual icefield of the Spider itself.

So everything was good: John was feeling fit, despite his coughing; the Spider, another key-point on the Face, had been reached; the weather was perfect and the forecast was for three more good days. They felt ready for the summit, readier than at any time before, ready to give the month of effort its proper climax.

At 3.45 a radio call from Scheidegg was due. Peter's voice came over loud and clear: 'Scheidegg to Eiger, Scheidegg to Eiger, how do you read, how do you read? Over.'

John picked up the radio: 'Roger, Pete.' He gave the news about Layton and Jörg Lehne. 'We're getting ready for the final push. We've sorted out our three days of food and we're planning on prusiking up the ropes in the morning and blasting for the summit. I hope you've got a good weather forecast for us. Over.'

There was a pause. 'Hello, John,' said Peter. 'Roger that.' There was another pause, and Peter came back in. 'Regret to state that preliminary weather reports from Zürich and Geneva say that there is a cold front approaching: this should arrive some time tomorrow night. Regret a cold front arriving some time tomorrow night. We are checking this. But it does not look good. Over.' There was despair in his voice.

John and Dougal swore violently. 'Christ, when are we going to get a break?' asked Dougal rhetorically. John spoke into the radio again – his elation had gone. He asked for more details of the front. 'God, we're fed up,' Peter told him. John and Dougal now discussed what they should do. But as John told Scheidegg by radio, there was really only one option: 'We'll just have to sit it out until we get a good forecast.'

Apart from their assault rations, they had enough food for three days of waiting. They decided, hopefully, to stick to their plan of going to the summit, in case there was a change in the weather forecast. If the weather forecast was confirmed in the next morning's radio call, they would simply have to stay where they were. Just at the end of the afternoon call Layton came back to the bivouac after roping down from the Spider. He was happy at the progress he, Jörg Lehne and Karl Golikow had made. But he was as disappointed as the others when they told him about the forecast.

John asked him if it would be possible to set up another camp in the Spider and use that as the take-off point for the summit when the good weather came. Layton said he didn't think it would be. He also said that he and Jörg Lehne had looked at the ice bands that both teams had thought of traversing to reach the Fly, and that they looked very difficult. It would be better to try a traverse line higher up.

Chris and Mick had spent that Monday on the West Flank making a reconnaissance climb for their photographic coverage of the summit push. In the rush to leave in the morning Chris forgot his crampons, and this and the deep powder snow made it a hard day. It was Mick's first day's climbing since the previous summer. Late in the afternoon they reached the shoulder of the West Ridge, about three-quarters of the way up, and it had been dark for two hours by the time they got back.

Both on the Face and at Scheidegg the postponement of the summit push meant a subdued evening.

The climbing team spent a comfortable night. Spring was approaching and the sun had begun to reach the Death Bivouac in the afternoon: the walls of the snow-cave were even thinner than before. But by now John and Dougal were hardened to their exposed situation.

On the morning of Tuesday 22 March John made the usual radio call to Scheidegg, anxious to learn whether there was any change in the forecast. There was: it was only a small change, but it could be important. 'There now seem to be two cold fronts,' Chris told John. One small one was due that night and would bring only light snowfall; the bulk of the bad weather would arrive with a second and larger cold front, due over the Eiger the following night. John said his plans were still not to go to the summit that day; they would go as high as they could on a reconnaissance climb, with the possibility in mind of setting up a camp on the Spider.

Chris suggested he or Mick should climb up to the First Band with a rucksack full of food so that the summit team would have more than three days of standby rations. The obvious man to fetch the sack from there was Layton, because of his speed. But Layton said if he was going down to the First Band he would prefer to go all the way and perhaps have a day's rest at Scheidegg. John thought this was sensible, particularly if there was a danger they were in for another long, storm-battered siege.

Another problem had cropped up on the mountain. 'Chris, we're all in a quandary up here about the shovel you had,' said John. 'Did you leave it down below, or did you lend it to the Germans, or what?'

Chris thought long and hard. 'I'm sorry, John, my mind's an absolute blank about it.'

'Roger absolute blank,' said John. (The shovel was eventually found in the Fly – 'which means,' said Dougal, 'he must have given it to the Germans.')

So there it was: after all their preparations, all the anticipation, and despite the good weather, the summit push was off. Snow was forecast that night: the forecasts had been inaccurate before, but as John said, 'You can't stake your life on their being wrong.' To make things worse, none of the forecasters was prepared to predict the end of the bad spell. After a month of effort success seemed as remote as ever.

After the call the three climbers discussed what to do about supplies, and they decided that Layton should go down to Scheidegg. He was feeling a little jaded after his burst of activity below the Spider and they thought he might as well stay down until the weather got good again. Six days' supplies for three men would keep John and Dougal going for a long time, so they told him not to come back until the summit push was definitely on.

Layton left soon afterwards, and John and Dougal moped around unhappily, trying to decide whether to make a reconnaissance climb to the Spider or to sit in the snow-hole and save their energy. They finally decided to go to the Spider to make a supply dump there. They would leave after the radio call at 11.45 a.m.

Later that morning Mick went on to the terrace to look through the telescope. He swung it up to find the Germans' high point. There was a figure in the Spider, and a rope going up above him that was lost where it disappeared into the rocks. Mick pointed the telescope higher; and there, walking carefully but easily, was a climber in the ice of the Fly! He called Peter to look, and then they excitedly told the others: it meant that the climbing from the Spider to the Fly was easier than anyone had dared hope. If only their team were climbing, they thought: it must be worthwhile making some progress before the bad weather came.

The Scheidegg people gathered in Peter's room for the 11.45 radio call. 'Hello, John, I read you loud and clear,' said Peter. 'The first piece of information we have for you is that there is a German in the Fly. Repeat, there is a German climber in the Fly.'

John and Dougal looked at each other excitedly. 'Very good,' said John to Scheidegg. But there was better to come.

Peter continued: 'We have four weather forecasts for you. The cold front is just as strong, but it has slowed. The forecasts mostly agree that it will not now arrive until tomorrow night.'

For John and Dougal this news, together with the information about the German reaching the Fly, was like the lifting of a great black cloud. They looked at each other and smiled with relief. Suddenly everything had become clear. They could get to the Fly that night, bivouac there, and go for the summit the next day. With luck they would reach the top before the bad weather came. But at least they would be able to get out the next morning, no matter how bad the storm. Dougal began to repack his rucksack.

At Scheidegg Peter and Chris wanted them to go for the summit too. Not realising the decision was already made, Chris guardedly asked: 'John, what exactly are your plans now?'

Almost as guardedly John replied: 'This news that someone is on the Fly might change things.'

'Certainly the progress they've made up to the Fly is fantastic,' Chris said. 'It must be quite easy up to there.'

'So it would seem,' said John, 'and it's only a day out of there. I'm thinking we might modify our plans and go just as high as we possibly can with the idea that we might be able to climb all the way out to the summit tomorrow.'

Chris and John discussed it: Chris said there was every reason to go to the Fly that night – if the bad weather came early they could simply retreat to the Death Bivouac; if it came late they would be extremely well placed to reach the summit. 'It certainly looks very hard above the Fly but I don't think you can tell until you're actually rubbing your noses on it.'

John was only too happy to have Chris's agreement. He spoke the fateful words. 'Well then, I guess we'll alter our plans. Apologise to Layton that we've pushed off like this, but I think he'll understand.' Layton was to join in with the second German team going for the summit – before he had set off back to Scheidegg he had said he would be prepared to do this if the need arose.

Guido Tonella, the Geneva-based Italian journalist who knew John well, was in the room, and he told John: 'I'll come tomorrow with a bottle of champagne.' Peter arranged the time of the next radio call. 'Stand by at 3.45,' John told him. 'But we're going to be working awfully hard and I don't know if we're going to be able to make that broadcast.' Peter asked John how he was feeling and John replied, 'Real great.' Then he said: 'OK, Pete, I gotta get going. Anything else? If not, Eiger out.' 'No,' said Peter, 'just go, go, go, and we'll see you on the summit.' Several people yelled 'Good luck' and Peter said, 'Scheidegg out.'

It was true, it was really happening, they were actually going for the summit. They would be there the following night, and if not, the morning after. The days, the weeks of waiting, of tension, of decisions, of frustrations, were coming to an end. John and Dougal were leaving the Death Bivouac then, that very moment. They would climb up the ropes to the Spider and then on to the Fly, and the next day they would be making a route where none existed up the summit cliffs and the Summit Icefield. They would reach the top and then they would come down and talk and laugh and have baths and eat meals and sleep in beds. They would be able to look up and see where they had been, up that straight line that started in the snow slopes at the foot of the Face and finished on the summit, the line that meant that the Eiger North Face direct, the last great challenge in the Alps, had been climbed.

# Chapter VIII

At 3.15 that afternoon Peter went on to the terrace of the hotel to see how far John and Dougal had climbed. The x 33 lens of the telescope was focused on the Death Bivouac. He swung the telescope up the line of the route to the Spider. Suddenly, in a chill, chill moment that turned the world upside down, he saw a figure dressed in red falling through the air clear of the Face. It was stretched out and was turning over slowly, gently, and with awful finality.

Peter cried out desperately, involuntarily: 'There's someone falling, there's a man falling !' He tried to follow the figure but it disappeared behind a buttress. He jerked the telescope to the bottom of the buttress, just to the left of the Death Bivouac, but in time only to see chunks of snow tumbling out of the couloir. A climber was at the Death Bivouac, near the bottom of the couloir. To Peter he seemed transfixed by what he must have seen. The climber then moved slowly back to the Death Bivouac.

There were three other journalists on the terrace: Guido Tonella of the *Tribune de Genève*; Rudi Rohr of the Swiss tabloid *Blick*; and Hugo Kuranda, the Geneva stringer of the London group Associated Newspapers Ltd. All three hurried to the telescope.

'What did you see?' asked Tonella. 'Did you see limbs? Could it have been a rucksack or an anorak?'

'I saw a figure, stretched out, falling,' said Peter.

Kuranda looked through the telescope casually and strolled back to the other end of the terrace. Rudi Rohr fetched Fritz von Almen. He and Guido Tonella remembered seeing a climber on the fixed ropes below the Spider. There was none there now.

The terrace was immediately below the fourth-floor room that Chris was now sharing with his wife Wendy. Peter went to below the window. 'Chris! Chris Bonington!' he shouted up. Chris shouted something from inside the room. 'Chris, come down here,' Peter called back.

Chris arrived on the terrace a couple of minutes later. 'Come and look through the telescope,' said Peter for want of anywhere more secluded to take him. As Chris bent to look through the lens Peter, trembling, spoke quietly into his ear.

'I think someone's fallen, Chris. I'm pretty sure it was someone. I don't know who it was.'

Chris looked at him blankly. The two of them walked round the corner from the terrace and Peter told Chris what he had seen.

Chris asked: 'Could it have been a rucksack?'

'It could have been, Chris. But I don't think it was.'

Fritz von Almen had trained the telescope on the foot of the Face and started searching. In a few moments he found what he was looking for. A dark, huddled mass lay in the snow about 500 feet below the start of the fixed ropes. For a wide area around were spread pieces of equipment, their colours bright against the snow. Chris looked through the telescope too. He was sure the dark shape was a body. And then, in a deathly moment of recognition, he saw a blue rucksack lying nearby – the colour of the one John had been carrying.

Up on the bivouac ledge in the Spider were two figures in red and one in blue and red, obviously unaware that anything had happened below them. The two in red could be John and Dougal, Peter thought. But the German climbers were wearing red too. Chris, however, was sure that it was John.

'There's just a chance that he's still alive. We must get there quickly.'

Peter wanted to go with him. 'I'll go with Layton,' Chris told him. 'You stay behind and do what needs to be done here.'

Chris met Layton coming down the stairs from his room. 'Chris said he thought someone had fallen but he was hoping it wasn't John,' Layton said afterwards. Layton in turn went to look through the telescope at the shape in the snow, but thought it was only a bivouac sack.

There was a radio call due at 3.45. John had said during the 11.45 call: 'Stand by for a 3.45 broadcast. But we're going to be working awfully hard and I don't know if we'll be able to make it.' Yet the two figures in red standing in the Spider were certainly in a position to make a radio call. Precisely at 3.45 Peter attempted to make contact: 'Scheidegg to Eiger, Scheidegg to Eiger, how do you read, how do you read? Over.'

There was only the crackling of radio silence. John always carried the walkie-talkie himself when he was on the Face. Peter kept the radio on until 4.00, but he had known within a minute what the silence meant – just as he had known, despite the doubts that others had tried to inspire in him, that it was a man he had seen falling down the Face.

Chris and Layton left at 3.50. They skied down to the bottom of the Salzegg ski-lift. They used it to get up to the bottom of the West Flank and then started to traverse across below the Face. Chris had a radio with him. Peter stood by the telescope and guided him towards the shape lying in the snow.

At 4.30 they had reached a rock buttress about 300 yards from the shape. 'We suddenly had an immense feeling of relief,' Chris said afterwards. 'There was all this equipment spread around and we were sure it was just another piece.' 'I still thought it was a bivouac sack,' said Layton. Peter kept his radio open. Five minutes later it crackled alive. On the air came Chris, sobbing. 'It's John. He's dead.' He and Layton sat down in the snow and cried.

Peter was in Fritz von Almen's study. He tried to think of all there was to be done before the situation took hold of him. 'We must have guides to fetch the body,' he told von Almen.

'Tell them to take the body down to the railway line,' von Almen said.

'They can't,' said Peter. 'It would be too heavy, and ... they can't. We must have guides.'

'They should take it down themselves. Radio to them,' von Almen insisted.

Peter, despite himself, radioed to Chris. 'We can't, Pete, we can't,' said Chris, distraught.

'I'll telephone Schwendener myself,' Peter told von Almen. The hotel owner shrugged his shoulders and rang Hans Schwendener, Grindelwald's chief guide, to ask for a party to fetch the body.

After Fritz von Almen had gone out, Peter sat in the room for a time. Several people passed by outside, presumably journalists going to the telescope. Desperate to avoid them, he opened the door of the room and went down to the telephones in the hotel lobby. He and Chris had already sent Wendy off to Leysin in case the falling figure was John. She was to ring up *en route* to find out if it was.

But by chance Don Whillans had phoned from Leysin earlier, after Peter had seen someone fall but before he knew who it was. At 5.00 he phoned again. 'It's John,' said Peter. 'He's dead.'

'You're absolutely sure?' asked Don.

'Yes,' said Peter.

'There's nothing to say, really, is there?' said Don.

Since Wendy would not reach Leysin for several hours, Peter asked if he would tell Marilyn, and Don said he would. He and his wife Audrey arrived at the Harlin chalet ten minutes before the Swiss radio gave the news. Almost at once people began walking up the road to the chalet.

Immediately after he had seen John fall, Peter had looked through the telescope at the figures standing in the Spider. They were obviously unaware that anything had gone wrong. There was a great gulf between Peter and the climbers perched on their bivouac ledge. If only he could shout across that vast expanse of air ... Instead, it was to dawn on them gradually and agonisingly that John had fallen. What was going through their minds?

Here Dougal tells his story of the accident, from the moment at midday when he and John left the Death Bivouac for what they believed was the final summit push.

The sky was deep blue and the yellow line of the fixed rope glittered brightly against the dull black ice of the Third Icefield. It was a day for appreciation. I felt I was on the way to the completion of my greatest dream. The many years of hard-won experience were at last going to be put to as searching a test as one could find in the climbing world.

John and I had become very close friends on the previous trials. There was no other person with whom I wanted to share this unique experience.

I was ready first and quickly moved on to the first fixed rope. It was a great pity that Layton had gone down, but we had radioed for him to come back straight away and join Peter Haag and the second German assault party. Sigi Hupfauer was ahead of me on the ropes taking up supplies. We worked as a team. He would shout down when he was off the fixed line and I would start.

I was just starting the overhanging prusik up the side of the Pillar when John came round on to the Third Icefield. The prusiks were nasty – mostly free, which meant spinning with the heavy pack. The one above the Pillar was particularly bad. I swung violently whenever I left the Pillar. It was completely free for 100 feet and all the strain on the small 7-millimetre rope was over one piece of flat slab. I was happy to move on to the non-vertical section leading to the Spider.

It was a happy scene sitting on the tiny ice step at the foot of the Spider. It seemed unreal to be casually sitting talking in winter at such a moment in mountaineering history. I was with Roland Votteler and Sigi Hupfauer. Jörg Lehne was just starting yet another overhanging prusik up to the Fly. Jörg had found a relatively easy traverse line out from the top right corner of the Spider and had then dropped a rope straight down over the avoided overhangs. An hour passed and there was still no sign of John. There were no serious doubts as yet. Only small things which crept in. John should have been only half an hour behind. That was the usual time between two men prusiking at roughly the same rate. Of course, the bronchitis could still have been troubling him. He could have stopped to talk to one of the Germans. But there was also a reason we did not want to consider.

Another hour passed and Sigi departed for the Fly. Terrible thoughts began to pour into my mind. I shut them out. I could sense the same thing happening to Roland as we talked. There was no point in discussing it. Such fears are best kept under control. They can cause panic measures if let loose.

Roland was due to go down to the Death Bivouac so he started abseiling, intending to find out what was wrong and to tell John that I had gone on towards the Fly.

It was hard to control my fears on the long, spinning prusik. I had reached the top and was securing my rucksack when I looked down. There was a figure on the rope. Sudden terrific elation swept through me. Then shattering depression. It was Roland. He was shaking his head, too overcome to speak. I abseiled back down, scarcely aware of swinging until I crashed into the ice of the Spider.

Roland told me that the rope had broken near the top of the prusik from the Pillar. There was a faint possibility that it had broken when John was just starting up it and he had not fallen. There was the even more unlikely one that he had fallen and survived. These vague hopes were completely shattered as Sigi Hupfauer, who had been in touch with Scheidegg by radio, came to the top of the rope from the Fly and shouted, 'John's dead.' We didn't speak. There was nothing more to say. A broken rope, and gone was one of my greatest friends and one of Europe's best mountaineers.

It was now almost dark and Roland and I prepared to bivouac where we were. There was only one problem. My rucksack with all the bivouac gear was at the top of the fixed rope leading to the Fly. I had no alternative but to go up for it. It was one of my worst moments. My heart was just not in it. It needed a ferocious effort of concentration to keep myself from making stupid mistakes. Descending was worse. I had not only mental but physical troubles. The rope had cut through the neck of my parka and for more than half the abseil it was rubbing on bare flesh. When I reached Roland he shoved some plaster on the wound. It was cold for him as all his down gear was at the Death Bivouac. I gave him my down jacket as I had a sleeping bag. There was no food. It had all gone down with John. But we had a cooker and some coffee, which we were in the act of preparing when there was a great scraping of crampons and violent twanging on the rope and Karl Golikow appeared like a ghost in the night. He had come down from the Fly to bring me a radio so that I could communicate with Scheidegg. A fine gesture. He put his arm round my shoulder and swore violently – something that meant more than any tears or words of commiseration. We three crawled into the tent sack, supped the foul paraffin-flavoured coffee, and talked.

When the first moments after the death had passed, with all their immediate problems, the most urgent thing for the people at Scheidegg was to make contact with Dougal, to talk to him, to tell him what was happening, to tell him he was not alone. John had been carrying the radio, but Harri Frey, ringing from Stuttgart, told Peter to go to the Stöckle restaurant and use the German radio link.

At 7.00 p.m. Peter spoke to Roland Votteler. Roland said that one of the ropes below the Spider had broken. Peter asked if he could speak to Dougal, but he was in the Spider without a radio. The Germans made contact with the Fly, and Karl Golikow very generously said he would take their radio down to Dougal so that he could talk to Layton, Chris and Peter.

After the accident the first reaction at Scheidegg was that the climbers must come down. To Chris there seemed no question of Dougal and Layton continuing, and he thought that the German team would have to come down as well. Harri Frey told Peter that his team would not go on. During the

German radio call at 7.00 Peter Haag also said he thought they should come down. But Jörg Lehne was not so sure … and gradually, as the initial shock passed, things began to appear in a different light. The same things were passing through Dougal's mind.

First thoughts for everyone had been to give up the climb and descend as quickly as possible. But once we had controlled our whirling emotions, rational thoughts began to come. Were we not poised in a position to achieve John's greatest wish? We could pay him no greater tribute than to go on and complete the climb. If complete, the route would be his memorial – the John Harlin Route. If incomplete, his last resting-place would be only another cross on the death lists of the critics. We would go on as an international rope united by the spirit of John. I knew full well that this would bring a shower of criticism on our heads, but I knew he would have wished us to continue, and we were sure that this was what Marilyn and his parents would want too. So who had the right to criticise?

At 9.00 p.m. I contacted Chris at Scheidegg on the radio. He agreed completely with the decision. He also said that Layton would start up first thing in the morning and try to come up to the Fly that day to join the summit team. We had been in the grip of a great depression, but once the decision was made we felt we had something to fight for again.

# Chapter IX

Wednesday 23 March was a cold day. The men involved in the climb took new stock of their situation. Layton left for the Face at 9.30, planning to join up with the four Germans at the Death Bivouac and to go to the summit with them. 'But I didn't have any feeling for the climb any more,' he said afterwards. 'It's not worth someone's life. And when it's someone you know ... '

Peter was continually visited by the image of a falling man, stretched out and dressed in red, turning over in the air like a falling leaf. It was some time before he could work out why the image seemed so wrong. One of the reasons why people climb is so that they can exercise complete control over themselves. On the mountain they are acting as free agents, making open, rational choices on their own behalf. Any action they take, any movement they make, even one on which their life depends, is something they have chosen to do. But John's death was the antithesis, the exact converse, of all this. He had not just made a choice of action, having evaluated the risks and complexities involved. He was climbing on the rope and it broke. There was nothing he, the most careful of climbers, could have done about it. It could have happened to any of the other ten men on the Face. It need not even have happened on the Eiger. It was a meaningless event.

After speaking at a press conference called by Harri Frey, Peter made radio contact at 11.45 with Layton, who had by now reached the Eigerwand station. Peter gave Layton the weather forecast – snow for Thursday. Layton said he hoped that everyone would be able to get out to the summit by the following night. If they reached the Summit Icefield before the snow came, they should be safe. 'You're doing fine, Layton,' Peter said. 'We're really feeling this down here now, but if you and Dougal get to the top it's going to make all the difference, it really will.'

Peter then went down to the hotel lobby. He was intercepted by Harri Frey, who said he had something to tell Peter in strict confidence. They sat huddled round a table and Harri said that Karl Golikow had been down that morning to inspect the fixed ropes between the Death Bivouac and the Spider. Karl had found at least six places where the ropes were frayed even worse than at the point where the rope had broken. The German team had decided that those of its members who were above the ropes should carry on to the summit, and those below should come back down.

Peter was at once very anxious for Layton. Harri said they had a radio call to the Face at 2.00 p.m. and Peter asked if Peter Haag could intercept Layton and tell him about the ropes. Just before 2.00 Peter went to look through the telescope. He could see Layton and he appeared to be preparing to prusik up the first fixed rope above the Death Bivouac. Peter raced to the telephone and called Harri Frey at the Stöckle restaurant. Harri was already talking to the Face. Peter tried to get a message through, asking him to tell Peter Haag to be sure to speak to Layton. Not sure whether he had succeeded, he went back to the telescope, and to his relief saw Layton arriving at the German snow-hole.

Layton was in fact paying a normal courtesy visit before prusiking on up to the Spider. But when he got into the hole the Germans mistakenly told him that Peter Gillman had said he was to come back down because the ropes were too bad. Peter had of course said no such thing: he merely wanted Layton to be told about the ropes so that he could make his own decision whether to carry on or not. The Germans explained that they weren't going on themselves and Layton said he would stick with them.

Ten minutes later Karl Golikow and Rolf Rosenzopf left the snow-hole to take supplies up to the Spider. When they were gone, Layton asked Peter Haag if he would like to go with him up the fixed ropes to the Spider and then on to the summit by the Exit Cracks on the normal route. They would belay one another on the fixed ropes, and by using the Exit Cracks they would leave most of the climbing ropes free for the summit team. Peter Haag said he would like to do this. But shortly afterwards Karl Golikow came back with all the ropes, which meant they could no longer get up to the Spider.

Layton was in two minds about whether he would have preferred to continue. 'I could have got up – it would have been worth it even if it had meant six months in hospital,' he said at one stage. But he had nearly had a touch of frostbite on the climb already, and would almost certainly have lost some toes if he had been caught in a storm higher up. He realised this, and decided in the end that he was better off not having gone on. 'That Face had killed enough people already. And then John … '

At 3.45 Peter went up to the German radio at the Stöckle to try to make contact with Layton. But Layton came through on his own set instead and spoke to Marie at Scheidegg. 'We'll be coming down in the morning and bringing the ropes down with us,' he said. Mick arrived and told Layton that he had seen Dougal and a German three rope-lengths below the ice leading to the summit, but that they hadn't moved for an hour. Layton knew where the leading climbers were already, and he also knew that those last 300 feet were extremely difficult climbing. 'You've done really well, lad,' Mick said. 'It's just hard luck. I'm sorry.'

All this time there had been no news from the five leading climbers themselves. What had been happening that morning? Dougal gives his own account.

The bivouac was long and cold, and occasionally little avalanches poured over our heads. But morning came as always, and we quickly prepared for our different tasks. Karl was to go down to re-establish the broken link; Roland to wait in the Spider to haul supplies. I started off on the loathsome prusik to the Fly.

I reached it, feeling my lack of food, to find Jörg Lehne, Günther Strobel and Sigi Hupfauer still in their bivouac. They all expressed their feelings of sorrow. Immediately I said that I'd had nothing to eat Sigi delved into a rucksack and produced some bread and chocolate, and Günther started the stove to make a drink. For the present it was stalemate. We could not climb any further until we had some more ropes. Karl and Günther had climbed 100 metres above the Fly on the previous day. Jörg prusiked up to the high point in the hope that by the time he had reached it the other ropes would have arrived. The rest of us sat on the little ice step and talked. It was a unique situation. Peering down at the tiny figures of skiers below made our position seem unreal. We were so close to civilisation and could see and understand what was happening, and yet they were so far removed from us. This could have been another world. For us it was. To reach the other again, we would have to find a way through the maze of ice-filled cracks and overhangs which surrounded us. It was a wilderness of rock, ice and snow – the trump card of the mountain which had already almost hammered us to defeat.

It would have been sufficient to have had this obstacle alone, but nature now piled on the lot. The clouds came down and by early afternoon it was snowing. We heard by radio that there were some spare ropes in the Spider, so Sigi went off to collect them. Günther and I just sat and got cold. Jörg was in a similar state 100 metres higher. Sigi was soon back and Günther set off with the ropes to Jörg. They were going to push as far as possible, fix the ropes and come back to the Fly to bivouac. Sigi and I set to work to make two decent platforms.

At Scheidegg Chris had been having a busy day. That morning he had gone with Layton to the foot of the Face. Then he and Mick had skied down to the police station at Grindelwald to identify John's body. He got back to Scheidegg to discover that the climbers were hoping to get out to the summit the next night.

Chris had been laying ambitious plans for taking photographs of their arrival. He hoped, for example, to rope 300 or 400 feet down from the summit to take pictures from alongside the climbers as they came up from the Summit Icefield. Now that the push was on he had to move fast. Already the cold front that had been over Paris the previous day was arriving; clouds were in sight over the mountains to the north and east. He telephoned Hermann Geiger, who promised him a helicopter in an hour's time.

Chris and Mick feverishly packed their rucksacks. They took with them two 100-metre lengths of rope for roping down from the summit and two long aluminium stakes for anchors. They had enough food and supplies for five or six days, and all their down bivouac gear. Chris stole Peter's crampons and then made Peter take them to the ski-shop next to the hotel to have them adjusted to fit his boots. Although the sky above Scheidegg was still almost clear, the first clouds had arrived, convening almost magically on the Face and hiding it from view.

At 4.15 the three-seater helicopter touched down on the snow just above the Suvretta hut and Chris and Mick bundled themselves and their three rucksacks into it. The pilot, it turned out, could speak no English, but fortunately Marie was on hand to explain where they wanted to go. She pointed dramatically at the Eiger and said, 'Au sommet, s'il vous plaît.' The pilot looked pained: 'Impossible.' But he shrugged his shoulders and took off.

By now the clouds filling the concavity of the Face were spilling on to the West Flank, where a strong wind waited to whip them away. In these conditions the helicopter was too light to go anywhere near the summit. The pilot flew to the bottom of the glacier that fills the saddle between the Eiger and the Mönch and pointed: that was as far as he could take them. Chris was appalled – he and Mick wouldn't be able to get anywhere near the summit from there, he thought. Reluctantly he asked to be taken back to Scheidegg. The pilot soared away from the glacier and headed back down.

On the way back they had an idea. Part of the problem was that they had three rucksacks of equipment. If they made a ruthless selection they could pack all that they wanted into two of the rucksacks and leave the third behind. They were now almost over Scheidegg again, so they told the pilot they wanted to go back. By now he clearly thought they were mad but at two pounds ten shillings a minute he presumably didn't mind. Into the third rucksack went one of the 100-metre ropes, the 16-millimetre ciné-camera, a stack of food, one of their two walkie-talkie radios – the wrong one, as it turned out – and, by mistake, three of the four gas-cartridges they had taken for their cooking stove. They also decided to abandon their aluminium stakes.

Chris managed to persuade the pilot to fly 500 feet up from the foot of the glacier. The glacier had a slope of about 30 degrees, too steep for the pilot to land. He hovered about six feet above the slope and there was nothing for it but to jump. Chris poised in the doorway. Suppose – just suppose – there was a crevasse under the innocent-looking snow? He shut the thought from his mind and jumped. There was no crevasse, and Mick followed. They had an overwhelming feeling of isolation as the helicopter wheeled away from them and dropped quickly back down to Scheidegg.

They had been put down about 2,500 feet below the summit of the Eiger on the glacier between it and the neighbouring Mönch. Their first problem was to get off the glacier and on to the Eiger's West Flank. They were on windslab, a frozen snow crust covering loose snow underneath: an extremely avalanche-prone combination. Every step forward sent cracks snaking in all directions across the snow around them.

By the time they got off the windslab they were both highly tense, it was getting dark, and Mick was very tired – it was only the third day after his arrival at Scheidegg. After a long push through tiring snow they found themselves on a difficult ice-pitch that had no real protection. This led to the top of a rock step somewhere on the West Flank, where it met the North Face. Below they could see a snowfield where they thought they should be able to dig a snow-hole. It seemed to be about 200 feet below and, a little nervously, they prepared to abseil down to it. Chris went first and to his delight found that in the dark they had absurdly misjudged the distance: the snowfield was only 40 feet down. Mick followed him, and when he landed on the snow found to his horror that for the first time in his life he had lost his ice-axe. In the past he had always been meticulous to see that it was securely attached to his waist-belt but his tiredness must have made him careless. They stumbled several hundred feet along below the wall they had abseiled down, and finally found a bulge of snow large enough for a snow-hole.

It was now 8.00 p.m., and completely dark. Chris started digging. Mick had a bad time of it because he had nothing to do except stand and get cold while Chris worked. But after half an hour there was enough of a hole for Mick to shelter inside. It took them until 11.00 p.m. to finish the hole and they got to sleep at midnight.

Meanwhile, Peter had been literally running around all day. After lunch he was met by a policeman from Grindelwald who had come up to Scheidegg to inquire about the accident. Peter battled through a description in German of what he had seen and then got involved in Chris's and Mick's preparations to leave for the West Flank. The policeman grabbed hold of him to sign his statement just as he hurried off up to the Stöckle to see if there was any news from the Face.

At 5.00 p.m. he spoke briefly to Dougal, who radioed rather mysteriously: 'We are at the end of obvious difficulties.' Dougal did not elaborate on this, simply adding that it was very cold and snowing. Peter came back down to Scheidegg. There he was met by an excited Guido Tonella, who took him to a recess in the hotel lobby and pointed dramatically at an orange rucksack. It was the one Mick and Chris had left in the helicopter. All that Guido knew was that the pilot had given it to him, saying that Mick and Chris didn't want it. Guido had brought it into the hotel and told the story to those journalists waiting there. The *Paris Match* man promptly emptied the rucksack, hoping to find, perhaps, that Chris had left his cameras behind!

Peter simply did not believe that Chris and Mick had abandoned the rucksack. Guido Tonella told him that they had had to jump from the helicopter and he formed a picture in his mind of Chris and Mick standing in the snow waving at the pilot to throw them the third rucksack, and of his misinterpreting this as a signal to take it away. He rang up Sion airport at once. 'It's unbelievable,' he told the girl who answered the phone. 'The rucksack contains all their food and rope. They must be in extreme danger by now.' He added, in a voice of high drama: 'We must get it up to them before it's too late.'

The girl promised to find out what had happened. An hour later he phoned again. Hermann Geiger was away but Peter spoke to his manager, who had the pilot with him. The manager said that Chris and Mick had sent the rucksack back. Peter simply did not believe this. He asked for the helicopter to come back at first light the next day. The first German television team wanted a helicopter as well and the manager promised that a helicopter would certainly come if conditions allowed.

But the forecast was not good. A storm was due that night. Peter felt anxious both for Chris and Mick and for the five climbers poised for a dash for the summit. The only news he had was the one message from Dougal that he was at the end of obvious difficulties. This sounded good: but perhaps it was too good to be true. The cliffs from the Fly to the summit were vast – nearly 1,000 feet of climbing. In the driving snow that had hit the Face at about the same time Chris and Mick had left for the summit it would be easy to be mistaken.

It turned out that this was in fact the case: as Dougal, with the benefit of hindsight, tells.

It was hard work digging the bivouac ledges. The ice was tough and Sigi Hupfauer and I had only a North Wall hammer and shovel. One of us carved while the other scraped out the debris. It took us a whole afternoon to carve out two platforms where we could at least sit in comfort, with legs over the edge.

We started cooking in the snow-filled twilight – ghostly figures round the flame. Small powder-snow avalanches hissed all around. There was suddenly a greater hiss and some stonefall, and Jörg came abseiling into the glow. He was quickly followed by Günther. They had been going well. Günther had led three more difficult rope-lengths, the only incident being a fall of six metres when one of his Fifi hooks had broken.

He reckoned he had been really close to the Summit Icefield. We all stood around drinking coffee, pleased by the news. It seemed we were above the obvious difficulties. Jörg made radio contact with base and then passed the radio to me so I could give my news to Peter. We departed to our respective steps in the ice. Jörg and Günther on the top floor, Sigi and I on the other. We had a struggle to crawl into our tent-sack, and taking off boots and crampons

# Chapter X

On Thursday 24 March Peter woke at 6.00 a.m. and looked out of his bedroom window. The Face was covered with cloud and a vicious wind was driving clouds of powder snow off the ridge just above the hotel. He got dressed and went downstairs. At 6.30 there was a call from the BBC morning programme *Today*; he answered questions for three minutes on the basis of the hope that the climbers would reach the summit that evening.

At 6.45 the German television team appeared, laden with rucksacks. They were hoping to be dropped on the West Flank by helicopter, and they said they would take the rucksack with them that Chris and Mick had left behind. But at 7.00 Geiger telephoned to say that flying was out of the question for the time being.

At 7.45 Peter, to his relief, made contact with Chris. He at once asked about the third rucksack. 'We'd love to have taken it,' Chris told him. 'We just couldn't carry it.' He assured Peter that they had enough food but that they would like their gas-cylinders if the German television team were coming up. Peter gave Chris the message from Dougal that the climbers had reached a point above obvious difficulties.

It was on the basis of this that Chris convinced himself that the climbers had reached the summit already. He and Mick left their snow-hole, which they discovered was about 1,000 feet below the summit and way over on the right-hand side of the West Flank. In a savage wind they battled their way up hard ice, cutting steps for a lot of the way. They reached the summit about midday.

Visibility was down to 50 yards and when they looked down the Summit Icefield they could see no one. But they found some orange peel and cigarette-ends just below the summit – for a moment they thought the climbers had come over the top already and they had missed them. Then Chris decided that the orange peel looked a good deal more than a day old. (He eventually discovered that it had been left by the German team when they climbed the Mittelegi Ridge that January.) It was as much as Chris and Mick could bear to wait on the summit for half an hour. At the end of that time they were both feeling the beginnings of frostbite, so they had to come down. They went 600 feet down the West Flank and decided to dig a new snow-hole, since the first one was so far from the summit. They still couldn't see into the Face from there as it was masked by cloud.

On the Face itself Dougal and his four companions had been laying the day's plans.

We had to get up by first light as it was going to be a long day. I stuck my head out hopefully to see if the snow had stopped. No such luck. It was a swirling grey dawn with visibility down to 30 feet. The ice-covered ropes seemed to float up into eerie nothingness. There was no breakfast, only a few pieces of chocolate. The cooker wouldn't work so there were no hot drinks. It was obvious that we would need Heibler clamps on the fixed ropes, as Jumars invariably iced up in such conditions. I cautiously eased my cramped limbs out of the tent-sack and set off down the ropes till I could shout down to the Spider. Poor Roland had spent the night in the Spider alone with three rucksacks. He was still in his tent-sack. I peered down into the hissing bowl of the Spider and shouted to Roland that we wanted some Heibler clamps. A little red figure appeared and said he would come up with them.

Günther came round and joined me. It was really vicious now. The wind had risen and was whipping the snow from all directions. No matter which way we turned it piled into our faces, freezing nostrils and eyelashes. Avalanches poured down continually. But our decision now was final. The previous day Karl and Rolf had brought supplies up to the Spider for the five of us in front. We were to represent the team. The others had considered it better that one team should make it rather than two fail.

The ropes going up to the Spider had been wearing badly and it seemed an unjustifiable risk for five heavily laden men to use them. Too much had been lost already. The section between the Death Bivouac and the Spider had already been stripped of ropes. We were to go for the summit with two leading light and fixing ropes, while the other three carried the supplies and took out the fixed lines. There was no thought of retreat. Storm or not, the way out was up. When Roland arrived from the Spider we would pull up the sacks and then take the rope with us.

Günther and I went back up to the bivouac, leaving the others to haul the sacks. He had been slightly frostbitten the day before and had a huge black blister on one finger. He did not feel like going ahead and we decided that I should prusik up to Jörg and carry on with him. The ropes were by now very badly iced. I had one Heibler clamp and four Jumars and still they managed to slip. Often I was left hanging on only one Heibler. Not a happy thought when one knows how easily they can slip sideways. As time was pressing I left my sack with all my sleeping gear hanging on a piton about 300 feet above the Fly. Moving more quickly, but still slowly because of the slipping Jumars, I reached a frozen Jörg standing half in slings on a tiny platform. I collected all the ironmongery and pushed on past Günther's high point into the unknown.

At 1.45 p.m. Peter radioed Chris again. 'We can't see any sign of them,' Chris said. 'It's pretty desperate up here; the wind's really savage.' Peter said he would go up to the Stöckle to see if there was any news from the Face.

When he arrived at the Stöckle he found the door locked which led from the restaurant to the bunkhouse where the Germans made their calls; it was some time before he could establish his credentials. Inside, he met Karl Golikow and Rolf Rosenzopf, who had come back from the Face that morning, the first climbers to do so since John's fall. They shook hands warmly. Karl produced from his pocket a small packet of tissue paper. Inside was a short length of blue rope (not Mammoth). One end had been cut neatly with a knife. The other was a mass of torn white strands – the place where it had broken.

Harri Frey had news for Peter. At 12.30 he had had a message from the Face to say that Jörg Lehne and Dougal were 40 feet below the Summit Icefield, but they had not made radio contact since. Harri was asking Jörg to press his transmitter button three times if he could hear Harri speaking. In response, Harri's radio crackled noisily three times. At least they were still alive …

Peter hurried back down to Scheidegg for the next call to Chris. 'I have big news, Chris. They are on their way. Two hours ago Dougal was 40 feet below the traverse leading to the Summit Icefield.' Without waiting for elaboration Chris called back, 'Right, out,' and went off the air. Peter thought Chris said 'Wait out,' and spent ten minutes trying to call him. Fortunately Bill Chipman, one of the dentists from Hahn air base, had recorded the message. He played it back six or seven times and finally established what Chris had actually said.

Chris had taken the message to mean that Dougal and the Germans would be reaching the summit that day. At once he and Mick packed their rucksacks and left to meet them. By now conditions were frightful, more savage than anything Chris had experienced before, even in Patagonia or the Himalaya. It was impossible to face into the wind – it was so cold and so strong that it seemed to bite into their flesh. For a second time they waited for half an hour on the summit but still saw no one so they came back down.

Peter was back at the Stöckle and Harri Frey told him that at 4.00 p.m. he had made out six words from Jörg Lehne: 'We are on the Summit Icefield.' At 6.45 Peter went outside into the howling wind with Wendy Bonington and radioed the news to Chris.

'I think the Summit Icefield is quite a big thing,' Chris said. He gave Peter instructions on how the climbers could reach the snow-hole. He said he would stick their red-bladed shovel in the snow outside. 'We've cut steps but they'd be difficult to follow. There's a complete white-out at the moment.'

John was to be buried at Leysin the next day. 'It doesn't look as though we're going to make the funeral now,' said Peter. 'I've sent some flowers from all of us. I think if you're on the Face I can't really leave here.'

By now the cold was cutting into Peter and Wendy. 'It's bloody shattering down here, so God knows what it must be like up there,' Peter said.

'It's really grim, it's desperate,' Chris told him.

Peter and Wendy fled into the warmth of the Stöckle. There they met Layton, who had just come back from the Face with Peter Haag and Günter Schnaidt. Layton said the descent in driving snow had been 'miserable'. 'It's hell up there,' he had told one of the dozen reporters who had surrounded him at Scheidegg. Bev Clark, who had flown out from England the day after the accident and spent the previous night at Leysin, also arrived. He and Layton were going to John's funeral. So the team would be represented.

On the West Flank Chris and Mick were digging into their snow-hole. When they left their first snow-hole that morning, expecting to meet the climbers on the summit, they had left most of their food behind. They thought of going back to fetch it but decided it would be too dangerous – it would have involved a traverse over unknown ground in darkness and the slashing blizzard.

They talked over their position. The shattering weather had made a very deep impression on them. Each time they had spent half an hour on the summit they had got deeply cold. They simply did not believe that the men on the Face would be able to climb in these conditions, and this meant they were in serious trouble.

But there was little that Chris and Mick could do to help. They had gone up to take photographs and they were lightly equipped. They couldn't reach their food and they were getting weak themselves. After a long discussion they decided it would be best if they came down to Scheidegg in the morning. They would be able to organise a rescue party and push back up the West Flank with food and equipment. If there was still no sign of the climbers they would rope down from the summit to look for them.

So the only people who knew what was happening in the hammering storm on the Face were the climbers themselves. That afternoon Dougal had gone into the lead.

The climbing was difficult. Hard mixed ground with poor piton cracks and always the storm in the background. I had to climb with bare hands at many places, but as yet my conditioning was proving its worth. Although I was cold, there was still no sign of frostbite. Less fortunately, as I reached a stance beneath a chimney there was still no sign of 'the end of obvious difficulties'. The difficulties above were still painfully obvious. I fixed the rope and Jörg came up and went through. He reached the top of a chimney with some effort but did not sound particularly happy about the ground ahead. 'It is still very difficult,' came floating out of the cloud.

A scraping of crampons, a few oaths, a great swing on the rope at my feet and Günther was up with me. While we had been involved in route-finding there had been a lot of good work going on below. Sigi and Roland had hauled up the sacks, then proceeded to climb to the point where I had left my rucksack, hauling all the ropes with them. Günther had brought two ropes with him. It was getting late. We could not notice approaching darkness as we had been climbing in half-light all day. Jörg ran out a full rope-length before he called me to come up. It had been a difficult pitch on ice-plated slabs. His stance was really poor. Only front-point footholds in the ice, with random poor pitons scattered to give an impression of protection. There was still no sign of the Summit Icefield. A rock buttress above and an icy ramp leading left were the only things visible. We discussed the way ahead. Günther came up. It was obvious that we would have to bivouac within the next half-hour. The only problem was where. We hadn't passed a decent bivouac site that day and there was certainly none visible just ahead. Also I had left my sack about 400 feet below.

Günther and Jörg had a tent-sack and down suits, so they decided to stay where they were. I knew that a night in the open without any bivouac gear would seriously weaken my chances of survival, so decided to abseil down to my rucksack and hope that Sigi and Roland had found a decent site. 'See you in the morning,' I said and slid off into the snowy darkness. Their goodnights followed me down the rope. I was alone with the swish of avalanches and howl of the wind – not the most comforting of companions. I reached the point where we had started climbing that day and there, just 100 feet beneath me, was a tiny red bivouac sack pinned to the ice. I quickly slid down to be greeted by the hum of the paraffin stove and Sigi and Roland, looking remarkably cheerful considering their bivouac site was an ice step 18 inches broad. They were sitting with the tent over their heads and were relying on their crampon points to keep them in balance. Fortunately they had dug out a similar platform about three feet lower, so at least I would be able to sit down that night.

A hand appeared out of the tent-sack with a can of soup. I was really grateful for something hot. It was the first for twenty-four hours. After that there was nothing else to do but go to my icy bed. It was a wild night. I was curled up with one leg on the step and one hanging. The tape sling under my outside arm kept me from sliding off. The tent-sack whipped violently in the wind and the powder-snow avalanches poured on to my covered head, finding their way through little rips in the sack. I could only manage to take my crampons off – I had to keep my boots on to keep in the footholds on the ledge. My sleeping bag was frozen solid and offered little warmth. The amazing thing was that I managed to doze for parts of the night. But the dozes did not last for long, as violent shivering fits constantly brought me crashing back to a realisation of the position. I was being subjected to the worst storm that I had ever experienced on a winter's night on the North Face of the Eiger.

# Chapter XI

At 6.00 a.m. on Friday 25 March Toni Hiebeler knocked on Peter's bedroom door and came in. 'Three of the German team and I are going up the West Flank to the summit. We will see if they need any help. Can you tell Chris to stay up there? Does Layton want to come?' Peter told him that Layton was going to John's funeral but that he would ask him. Outside there was a vicious wind, and swirling grey cloud filled the bowl of the Face. The temperature at Scheidegg was –12 °C.

After an early breakfast Peter went outside to radio Chris and was at once caught in a cloud of driven spindrift. 'Chris, do you read? Chris, do you read?' To his relief Chris came on the air promptly and Peter told him that four Germans were coming up the West Flank.

'We'll stay here, then,' Chris answered. 'We'll dig a snow-hole big enough for everyone.'

Peter asked if there was anything he wanted brought up. Chris started to explain: 'Yes, we'd like ... '. Suddenly his voice became a faint distorted crackle. Hard as Peter tried, he simply could not make out the words. 'Chris, I do not read you, Chris, I do not read you; please speak loud and slowly, please speak loud and slowly.' But the crackling remained tantalisingly incoherent.

This meant that Peter now had no way of telling whether and when the climbers reached the summit until the German party had forced a way through the blizzard up the West Flank. More seriously, it meant that Chris had no way of telling Peter where the new snow-hole would be and what he wanted brought up. Unless ... Peter remembered Harri Frey's instructions to Jörg Lehne the previous day. 'Chris, I cannot read you any more. If you can read me, please press your transmitter button three times.' There was a pause ... and then Peter's radio crackled alive for three long definite periods.

Peter thought quickly. He didn't know Morse code, even if Chris did. He would have to frame questions that Chris could answer with either yes or no – providing he could guess what Chris wanted to talk about. 'Chris, I will ask you questions. If the answer is yes, press the button three times. If it is no, press the button twice. Do you understand?'

Back came the answer – three long periods of crackling on his radio.

'Chris, will you be digging the new snow-hole below where you are now?'

The radio crackled twice.

'Will you be digging the new snow-hole above where you are now?'

The radio came alive three times.

Peter moved on to supplies. 'Do you want more food?' Two crackles.

'Do you want more gas-cylinders?'

Three crackles.

'Do you want more rope?'

Two crackles.

Peter remembered seeing a pair of crampon straps in the rucksack brought back by the helicopter pilot. 'Do you want crampon straps?'

Again two crackles.

'Chris, I will try another call in one hour's time. Do you understand?'

Three crackles.

'Peter to Chris, you're doing fine, over and out.'

Peter went to look for Layton and found him in Chris's bedroom, getting ready to go to Leysin. Peter asked him if he wanted to go up the West Flank with the Germans, but Layton said that as he didn't think he was absolutely necessary he would prefer to go to John's funeral. He couldn't find a shirt so took one of Chris's, which was far too small. 'Has anyone got a black tie?' he asked. Peter fetched him the tie he had borrowed from John to wear to Hilti von Allmen's funeral just eight days earlier.

In the hotel lobby Peter met Peter Haag, who was looking for an expansion bolt kit and some cooking pots for the West Flank party. The two Peters went through Layton's equipment and found the expansion bolts, but the only pot they could find was a battered, lidless kettle.

The next time Peter made a radio call he could just make out some of the words Chris spoke. Peter asked if there was anything else Chris wanted. 'Please repeat items six times.' He understood 'goggles' and 'gloves' at the first attempt, but then Chris said something that sounded like 'Du-bay-sok, du-bay-sok, du-bay-sok, du-bay-sok.' Chris said it over and over again and it wasn't until the fourth batch of six repetitions that Peter comprehended: 'Duvet socks.'

There were only ten minutes before the Germans were to catch the train from Scheidegg to Eigergletscher at the foot of the West Flank. Peter found several miscellaneous gloves in Chris's room, but despite a long, frantic search, no duvet socks. With one minute to go he hurtled into the sports shop next to the hotel, seized two pairs of goggles, and threw a 50-franc note on to the counter.

The four German climbers – Toni Hiebeler, Karl Golikow, Günter Schnaidt and Rolf Rosenzopf – were now on the train and he passed the things for Chris in through the window. '*Sie machen einen Bivouac unter dem Gipfel*' – 'They are making a bivouac below the summit' – he shouted to Toni Hiebeler as the train moved off.

In the meantime Chris and Mick had left their snow-hole and were climbing up towards the summit again. They stopped just short of the top and looked into the Summit Icefield, but there were still no climbers to be seen. They started looking for a place for the snow-hole. But every time they started actually digging they quickly hit ice or rock and kept moving further down the West Flank. Finally they found a bank of snow about 400 feet below the summit and set to work.

Layton and Bev Clark left Scheidegg on the 10.30 train to Lauterbrunnen. Martin Epp joined them at Wengernalp. He had lost two of his best climbing partners in a week.

Peter went up to the Stöckle to see if Harri Frey had made radio contact with the Face. He had tried incessantly but with no success. Peter decided to stay at the Stöckle to wait for news. One advantage the place held was that there were fewer journalists there: he had spent much of the previous evening denying one story that the climbers had given up, and another that they had already reached the summit. He rang Wendy Bonington and Joan Matthews and told them to come up too.

He sat at a table with Heiner Hepper of the First German Television Band. At the next table were Harri Frey; Peter Haag, who had been unable to join the West Flank team because he was suffering from fever; and a member of the Munich Bergwacht, Dieter Seel, who had come out at the time of the storm a week earlier. Periodically Harri would try to call Jörg Lehne on the Face, never with any success. But he was in touch with Karl Golikow on the West Flank. Karl's first message was that they were on to the Flank itself and that the snow was very deep.

Peter went outside a number of times to call Chris. Occasionally he could hear Chris's voice but he could no longer make out any of the words. Peter asked Chris to press his transmitting button three times if he could hear him, but there was no audible response to that either. Peter transmitted the news about the West Flank party in the hope that Chris could hear him. But there was nothing he could tell Chris about the climbers on the Face.

On the West Flank Chris and Mick were digging the new snow-hole. They could hear Peter well, and frantically pressed their speaker button three times whenever he asked them to. They were annoyed that he didn't give them any news – not realising that there was none to give.

Again, only the climbers in the raging storm on the Face knew what was happening. Dougal resumes his account.

Sigi and Roland kept shifting uncomfortably on their stance. They could not even take their crampons off. A vague greyness was the signal of day. Staying on the bivouac hadn't been too easy but preparing to leave it was really unpleasant. My gloves and gaiters were frozen solid. My numb fingers pulled ineffectually on the crampon straps. To add to my troubles, one of the straps broke. I then had painfully to extract a cord from my ice-coated rucksack and fix it to the crampons. This simple manoeuvre took over an hour.

Slowly my mind began to face up to the day. I started painfully prusiking up the ropes again. I hadn't thought it possible that the storm could get worse, but somehow nature managed to drag up her last reserves and throw them at the five miserable figures fighting for fulfilment of a dream. Half-way up the first rope my fingers started to freeze. There was nothing I could do to stop it. The hostile forces were insidiously beginning to win. I pulled off my gloves at the stance and was confronted with ten white wooden objects. The only thing to do was to take a super dose of Ronicol. This eventually began to take effect and I waited in agony for half an hour as the blood began to recirculate.

Then it was on with the gloves and up to our high point of the previous night. There was neither sight nor sound of Jörg and Günther. To my surprise, there was a gap of 40 feet between the end of one fixed line and the beginning of the next. Also to my surprise, they had taken all the ice-axes and hammers with them. For a long time I contemplated doing this stretch alone but eventually decided to wait for Sigi and Roland and lead it on a rope. It was perhaps fortunate that I did. Though not a very difficult pitch, it was not too easy without an axe.

I scraped up it and fixed the line for Sigi and Roland. The cloud suddenly parted for a few minutes and there were Jörg and Günther a rope's length ahead cutting up a 60-degree ice slope. This could be the Summit Icefield, I thought, but there was no indication of the summit or neighbouring ridges, so I decided not to be too optimistic and wait and see.

This was also a moment of revelation for Peter. A nervous lunch had passed. Between radio calls Peter was writing an article for the *Sunday Telegraph* called 'How to climb the Eiger'. The German group talked quietly. Outside the wind howled incessantly and clouds surged around the Face.

At 2.30 p.m. Peter happened to look out of the window. The clouds that had been boiling up and past the summit had cleared! He could see all of the Face above the Spider. There was a telescope outside and he, the two girls, the German party, and several journalists rushed to it. It was quickly focused on the Summit Icefield. Peter looked through it and there, through wraiths of cloud, he could see two climbers: they were on the icefield about 400 feet below the summit, and one was climbing while the other belayed him a short distance below. A little way below them were three other climbers.

They were visible for almost five minutes, and then the clouds closed in again. Everyone hurried in out of the cold. Peter had a wide grin, a mixture of relief and disbelief, the release after days of tension. He hugged Wendy and Joan. '*C'est incroyable*,' he told Harri Frey, '*incroyable!*' '*Formidable*,' said Harri.

The climbers were still alive. But their difficulties were certainly not at an end. Dougal was soon to be faced with the most nerve-shattering pitch on the whole climb, which he now describes.

About an hour after we saw Jörg and Günther, the three of us were gathered on a small stance in the centre of the icefield. There was a slight problem ahead – another gap in the fixed ropes. A slightly larger one this time: around 150 feet. The other two were out of sight again. There was nothing else to do but tackle the pitch.

The next hour was one of the most testing of my climbing career. It was 60-degree water-ice. The steps of the previous rope had been wiped out. I had no axe or hammer. My left crampon was wildly askew on my boot. The right one was loose. Armed with one dagger ice-peg, I moved off the stance. The wind was crashing the snow into my face with such force that it stuck in huge masses on my eyelids, making it impossible to see ahead. My movements were cautious and groping. I would search around for traces of a step, scrape it out, then make a breath-holding move up on my wobbly crampons. The pitch went on and on and I became increasingly aware of the extremeness of the situation. Sigi and Roland were on a very poor belay. There just could not be any question of falling. Yet in a strange way I was enjoying this test. I knew the odds were stacked with the house, but I felt in perfect control. There was no panic, only well-planned movement.

Fortune favoured me and I reached the top of the pitch. Slight trouble again, though. The rope I was aiming for was 20 feet to my left. I made a few tentative moves left, but came back quickly. There was no chance of doing it without an axe or some protection. A tension traverse[1] was the obvious solution, but on what? I could see only one solution and that was a terrible one to face. Down below I had once or twice tried to knock my ice-dagger into the ice with my Heibler clamp and had only succeeded in getting it in about an inch, which was no use whatsoever for protection. But it might stand the slight pull of a tension traverse. I didn't want to spend the rest of my days at that spot, so I knocked in the piton. It wouldn't go further than an inch. It also wobbled. Swallowing my heart, I tied the piton off,[2] fixed a sling and began the longest 30 seconds of my life. Point by point I edged across the icy slabs. There was no real point in worrying because it was out of my hands anyway. Three lives on an inch of metal. A last long reach and there was the rope. I quickly clipped on

---

1 Tension traverse – a traverse where the climber keeps himself in balance by using the pull of the rope against him.

2 Tie off a piton – tie a small loop round it where it enters the ice to reduce leverage, instead of fixing the sling to the hole in its head.

a Heibler, then hung, drained of everything by the terrific release of nervous tension. Then I tied off the rope for Sigi and Roland and prusiked on into the mist. I felt that somehow the summit must be near as the wind was now terrific in its intensity. It was almost impossible to breathe, far less see. Suddenly, through the storm I could make out two figures. My first thought was that they were Jörg and Günther; then Chris's voice came floating down. It was finished. The direct existed. There was no elation as I pulled on to the summit. Only a tremendous feeling of gratitude that Chris and Karl Golikow had come up to meet us.

There was no time to linger on the peak of my ambition. Chris led me down towards the snow-hole that he and Mick Burke had dug several hundred feet beneath the summit. The tension was over. I could happily stumble in someone else's footsteps. We cramponned downward in the never-ending storm. Suddenly there was a hole in the snow. I stuck my head inside into a different world. There was a happy chatter. Jörg and Günther were there, along with Mick, Toni Hiebeler, Günter Schnaidt and Rolf Rosenzopf. I lay down in a great daze at the sudden transformation. A brew of coffee came up from the depths of the hole. It was like no drink I had ever tasted. It provided the necessary link and slowly I began to unwind. My hands were blistered and useless, so I stuck them in my pockets while Günter Schnaidt unlaced my crampons.

About an hour later Sigi and Roland arrived with Karli. I hadn't realised how wild we must have looked until I saw them with the eyes of someone who was no longer fully occupied with the problems of the Face. Their clothing was ripped, their eyes sunken and wild. Eyelids, eyelashes, beard and nostrils were completely coated with ice but, incredibly, still smiling. It was a moving moment. The party was complete. Everyone began to relax after their appearance. The cooker hummed away with a never-ending supply of hot drinks. Food was passed round. Eleven people in a hole built for four. No national barriers existed here. We were united by the spirit of extreme climbing. The radio calls were lighthearted. Even when the oxygen gave out no one panicked. A shovel was quickly shoved through the entrance so that everyone could breathe and the cooker could function again. I was curled up between Chris and Karli. No one felt like sleeping so we talked the night away.

Spindrift kept blocking up the entrance, and oxygen was constantly a problem. But someone would always choke in time to shout, so that the life-saving shovel could be poked through.

Through the afternoon the anxious Anglo-German group at the Stöckle had been trying to make radio contact with the Face. Then at 5.00 p.m. Karl Golikow came through. 'Jörg and Günther are with me now, Jörg and Günther are with me now, *Ende Ende Ende.*'

Chris was up there with Karl. He had seen the West Flank party coming through the blizzard and had decided to go up to the summit to see if anyone was nearly there yet, leaving Mick digging out the snow-hole. When Chris arrived on the summit, he found Jörg and Günther and brought them down to where Mick was digging. Karl Golikow was there too and it was from here that he sent his radio message. Mick took Jörg and Günther down to the lower snow-hole as the one he had been working on wasn't big enough yet. Chris and Karl went back to the summit and looked over. Dougal was 60 feet below them, just ending the traverse to the bottom of the rope that hung down from an ice-axe plunged into the very tip of the summit. Dougal started up the rope and Chris called down. Dougal looked up and said, 'Christ, is that you, Chris?' Shortly afterwards he was up.

Chris took pictures of Dougal on the summit with his fourth camera – his first three had all frozen up when he had tried to take summit pictures of Günther and Jörg, and he had unrolled the fourth camera from his sleeping bag when he took them down to the top snow-hole. Now he took Dougal down, leaving Karl on the summit waiting for Roland Votteler and Sigi Hupfauer. Karl had to wait there an hour, and Roland was there for half an hour after he arrived, because no one went up to fetch him and the descent to the snow-hole alone would have been too dangerous in his condition.

At Scheidegg there was pandemonium. At the Stöckle there was only one telephone and Harri Frey and Peter monopolised that. The other journalists were torn between waiting at the Stöckle, the source of news, and returning to the hotel at Scheidegg where there were three telephones.

Peter spent the rest of the evening talking on the telephone: he spoke on Independent Television News bulletins, the BBC's *Twenty-Four Hours*, NBC News of New York. At 11.00 p.m. he was summoned to yet another call. He picked up the receiver expecting to hear his long-suffering wife Leni. Instead he found he was talking live on the BBC sound programme *Light Night Extra*.

There was little celebrating that night. Layton was at Leysin for John's funeral; Mick, Chris and Dougal were in the summit bivouac. Peter felt drained of energy and very tired. Between phone calls he sat quietly in the Gaststube with Joan, Wendy and Erica, the Swiss girl who ran Scheidegg's tiny post-office and who had helped the team whenever she could. 'We'll be going hell-for-leather for Scheidegg in the morning,' Dougal had said during the last call from the mountain at 9.00 p.m. Tomorrow, with the return of the climbers, was going to be another hectic day.

# Chapter XII

The morning brought fresh difficulties for the climbers squeezed into the snow-hole below the summit. All the summit team had frostbitten fingers, toes or both. Chris had to put on Dougal's crampons for him and Günther Strobel's as well. Dougal's feet felt cold but he didn't think they were affected. His hands definitely were. Huge black blisters covered three fingers on his right hand.

At last they were ready to go down. Dougal had been dreading this moment. Though not too difficult, even in summer the route down the West Flank is long, tedious and with a certain amount of danger, needing a high level of concentration. When they came out of the hole the weather seemed to be as bad as ever. Snow still crashed into their faces. But miraculously it was only spindrift: 100 feet below the bivouac the wind dropped and the cloud cleared. So much snow had fallen that the slabs that were so dangerous in the summer had been completely covered. The returning climbers just ran or slid through the deep snow.

Down at Scheidegg Peter had noticed them coming before breakfast. He got ready quickly and set off up to Eigergletscher with Heiner Hepper and his television team. A number of journalists had stayed at Eigergletscher overnight in the hope of stealing a march on their competitors. The weather was perfect: cold, still and sunny. Peter could see the climbers moving very fast down the West Flank, glissading long distances at a time. He and Heiner made a way through the ruck of journalists waiting just above the station and set off up through the snow.

The climbers had now disappeared from sight and there was a moment of puzzlement. Then suddenly they reappeared at the top of the slope above. In ones and twos they glissaded down, whooping and shouting, finishing up by ploughing in a great flurry of snow into the drifts at the bottom of the slope. Chris and Mick were first, and Peter was ahead of the other journalists. Mick ruffled Peter's hair. 'Good old Pete – out in front as usual,' said Chris. Peter handed out the beer he and Heiner had brought up. The eight German climbers arrived and so did Dougal, and he and Peter made their way back down to Eigergletscher.

There was a tumult of journalists and photographers waiting at the station. Mick and Chris tried to buy themselves some more beer; Dougal, helped by Peter, took off what clothes he could and left them on the platform. His hands were black but he said he could feel the circulation coming back. There was a train leaving and everyone piled into it, talking and laughing. A confused conductor edged his way through legs and rucksacks and Peter found himself buying dozens of tickets. At Kleine Scheidegg more people milled around the train as everyone climbed down. Peter had booked Dougal a room with a bath in the hotel and Dougal made his way to it. He left the red-bladed snow-hole shovel leaning against the hotel wall. It was never seen again.

Chris and Mick went up to Chris's room. Mick was very anxious as he took off his boots because his feet were wet. But he was relieved to find his feet undamaged. Chris was happy as he took his boots off: 'Look at that – these felt inners are completely dry.' He took his socks off and – horror: three of the toes on his right foot were completely black.

Staying at the hotel was the doctor who had treated Toni Kinshofer when he came off the Eiger after the first winter ascent in 1961, and he had a look at Chris and Dougal. He put some cream on their wounds and dressed them.

Now that everyone was down there were a great many things to be done. There was equipment to be sorted out. Everyone had been looking forward to dividing up the expedition gear, but most of this, and most of each climber's personal gear, had been left on the mountain. Even Peter's sleeping bag, which he had brought in case the hotel was full up with skiers, was now in one of the snow-holes on the Face. Max Eiselin, from whose shop in Lucerne they had bought most of the extra equipment they needed during the climb, was owed over £200 and the equipment that hadn't been used had to be taken back. There were bills to be paid in Interlaken, Grindelwald, Scheidegg and Wengen.

The weather stayed fine in the afternoon, and shortly after lunch four of the German team came down to the station to catch a train for Interlaken. Roland Votteler, Günther Strobel, Jörg Lehne and Sigi Hupfauer were all suffering from frostbite and had arranged to go into hospital. The two teams mingled on the station, shaking hands, exchanging addresses, taking photographs, and then posed together for a group picture. Tourists and journalists jostled for good positions. Then the four Germans climbed into the train and left.

They went first to Interlaken and then into a hospital near Stuttgart. Several weeks later came the terrible news that Roland Votteler and Günther Strobel had had all their toes amputated. 'Günther and Roland are accepting their fate with remarkable calm,' Karl Golikow wrote in a letter to Peter. Jörg Lehne lost the big toe of his right foot. The only member of the German summit team unscathed was Sigi Hupfauer.

Chris and Dougal were luckier. When they flew home they both went into the London Hospital, where they spent hours every day in long torpedo-shaped cylinders filled with oxygen at two to three times the normal atmospheric pressure. A month later they were discharged, both on their way to complete recovery.

On that Saturday evening, 26 March, the snow and wind returned to Scheidegg. Chris had to stay in bed but Dougal, Peter and Mick made their way up to the Stöckle for a farewell drink with the Germans who were still there: Peter Haag, Karl Golikow, Günter Schnaidt and Rolf Rosenzopf. The evening was subdued but happy: climbing plans for the summer were quietly laid and a certain amount of beer and wine was drunk. At midnight, the British party said goodbye and battled through the snowdrifts and biting wind back to the hotel.

On Sunday Peter and Dougal drove to Leysin. They called at John's pinewood chalet high up on the side of the valley. There they met Marilyn Harlin and her two children Andrea and Johnny, and John's parents. Later in the afternoon Layton, Mick and Bev Clark came too. That evening they all dined at a French restaurant in Leysin. It was Marilyn's first meal since the accident. After dinner Peter, Dougal and Mick went to the Vagabond Club, where they met Don.

The next day Peter and Dougal started back to Kleine Scheidegg. But first they drove west out of Leysin, along a narrow winding road through a pine forest, to Leysin's cemetery. They found John's grave quickly, a blob of colour on a grey-green background. The fresh earth was covered with flowers and wreaths, bedraggled after a day of rain: they were from John's family, the Swiss guides, business associates and his friends. Peter and Dougal stood there for a few moments without looking at each other. Then they walked quickly back down to the car. Below the cemetery the valley slopes fell down towards the Rhône, glistening in the sun and curving away through the mountains to the south. On the other side of the Rhône rose the foothills and the mountains and the peaks of the Chamonix range, capped with snow and streaked with cloud, watching, powerful, silent.

# Technical Description of Route

For pure ice, Scottish gradings (I–V) are used;
for mixed rock and ice, standard gradings (I–VI).
Go across snowfields to prominent couloir to left of first pillar
and almost directly beneath Eigerwand station.
Start in couloir. (Ice gradings I–V)

PITCH

| | | |
|---|---|---|
| 1 | Climb a steep ice pitch (70°). (IV) | *100 feet* |
| 2 | Go left on snowfield 30 feet, then up ice (70°–80°) for 70 feet to snowfield. (IV) | *100 feet* |
| 3–8 | Follow snowfield 50° to foot of the next steep section. | *ca. 800 feet* |
| 9 | Go up narrow couloir to the left of the rock buttress ice (75°), then traverse right on poorly iced slabs to stance on snowfield. (III sup.) | *100 feet* |
| 10 | Climb steep ice (75°–85°), treading first slightly left then straight up to bolt belay. (IV sup.) | *120 feet* |
| 11 | Move left 70° for 20 feet, then climb iced corner (90°) for 30 feet to icefield. (IV sup.) | *50 feet* |
| 12–13 | Up icefield 50°. | *200 feet* |
| 14–16 | Continue on steeper icefield (60°) with small steep steps (III) for 3 rope-lengths to beneath gallery window. | *400 feet* |

END OF FIRST SECTION

| | | |
|---|---|---|
| 17 | Go up to the right of the station window to a bolt stance. Belay in slings. 80 feet. (A3) | *80 feet* |
| 18 | Go straight up for 30 feet, then traverse 20 feet right into a diedre; climb this for 30 feet then come 20 feet right to beneath a smooth bulge. Climb the bulge to another sling stance. (A3) | *120 feet* |
| 19 | Climb a very strenuous overhang above the stance, then more easily to sling stance at top of First Band. (A3) | *100 feet* |

| | | |
|---|---|---|
| 20 | Climb steep ice (70°) with a few bulges. (IV sup.) | *60 feet* |
| 21 | Continue on this ice with odd bulges to stance on slab. (IV sup.) | *120 feet* |
| 22 | Go straight up on difficult mixed ground to a snowfield. (V–V sup.) | *40 feet* |
| 23 | Climb the snowfield for a rope-length – 2nd bivouac cave. | *100 feet* |
| 24 & 25 | Climb First Icefield. | *300 feet* |
| 26 | Traverse right at top, then back left to poor crack which leads to prominent gully system on Second Band. | *140 feet* |
| 27 | Climb crack. (V) | *40 feet* |
| 28 | Traverse right on snow. | *100 feet* |
| 29 | Climb the gully above – poor snow with ice steps. (III) | *120 feet* |
| 30 | Go up the chimney with rotten snow on left of stance. (V sup., VI – crux of Band) | *50 feet* |
| 31 | Traverse left on steep ice to top of Band – 3rd bivouac cave. (III sup., IV) | *100 feet* |
| 32 | Climb steep ice above arête at top of Band to stance beneath lower left end of Flatiron. (IV) | *140 feet* |
| 33–34 | Traverse right under the base of the Flatiron. | *250 feet* |
| 35–38 | Go up Second Icefield on right of Flatiron. Mainly snow with occasional steep ice steps. | *500 feet* |
| 39–40 | Traverse 200 feet right on snow and ice. | *200 feet* |
| 41 | Climb V crack on ordinary route to ice pitch. Belay above. | *100 feet* |
| 42–43 | Go up rotten ice to top of Flatiron. | *160 feet* |
| 44–45 | Traverse left to crest of Flatiron – Death Bivouac. | *300 feet* |
| 46 | Go round corner from Death Bivouac on mixed ground, then straight up Third Icefield on hard water-ice (60°) to ice-peg belay. (III) | *140 feet* |
| 47 | Continue to top of Third Icefield. | *100 feet* |
| 48 | Climb mixed ground to crest of arête leading to the Central Pillar. (V sup.) | *100 feet* |
| 49 | Go up the crest to stance on right side of Central Pillar. (III) | *100 feet* |
| 50 | Traverse left on aid to bolt and belay on sling stance at left end of Central Pillar. (A3 sustained) | *100 feet* |

| | | |
|---|---|---|
| 51 | Climb thin ice groove of sustained difficulty to bolt belay. (IV sup.) | *100 feet* |
| 52 | Go up ice trough to top of Central Pillar. (IV) | *80 feet* |
| 53 | Go along the narrow neck which connects the Central Pillar to the main face for 30 feet. Climb crack system above starting in a roof to sling and bolt stance. (A2 sustained) | *140 feet* |
| 54 | Go straight up above the stance on mixed artificial and free climbing for 100 feet (A2, V) | *100 feet* |
| 55 | Traverse right into ice grooves and climb these to the foot of the arête at the bottom of the Spider. (III) | *100 feet* |
| 56–57 | Go up the Spider to the start of a traverse line leading out of the right side. | *200 feet* |
| 58–60 | Traverse rightwards on mixed ground for three pitches to the Fly. | *300 feet* |
| 61 | Go up Fly to top left corner. | *100 feet* |
| 62–64 | Three pitches on mixed, loose ground to foot of prominent chimney system. (IV and V sustained) | *300 feet* |
| 65–66 | Climb the chimney in two pitches to an awkward stance. (V, V sup. Steps of A1) | *200 feet* |
| 67 | Go up behind stance to overhang, then traverse right to stance at the foot of chimney. (V, V sup. Steps of A1) | *130 feet* |
| 68 | Climb the chimney for 40 feet, then move diagonally left on icy slabs to poor stance at the foot of a leftward sloping diagonal fault. (V sup.) | *130 feet* |
| 69 | Follow the fault to its end on mixed ground. (V) | *80 feet* |
| 70 | Move back right and up for 100 feet on icy slabs. (V sup.) | *100 feet* |
| 71–72 | Up Summit Icefield on water-ice. | *300 feet* |
| 73 | Go left from stance round rock bulge and straight up to the summit. | *150 feet* |

# Glossary of Climbing Terms

*abseil* (German: 'to rope down') – a method of descent. The climber slides down a rope fixed at the top. He controls his descent by passing the rope round his body or through a friction device.

*artificial climbing* – the climber makes progress by hammering in pitons or bolts, hanging étriers from them, and standing up in these. This contrasts with free climbing, where only natural hand- and foot-holds are used.

*belay* – a climber belays when he anchors himself to the mountain, normally by tying a knot into his rope and passing it round a spike of rock or fastening it to a piton with a karabiner. Belaying is particularly important when the partner on the rope is climbing: if the partner falls, the belayed man will be able to hold him without being pulled off himself.

*bolt* – used in artificial climbing or to secure a belay where there is no crack for a piton. The climber has to drill a hole for the bolt first.

*cagoule* – large, loose waterproof jacket that pulls over the head instead of opening up the front

*Chromolly* – chrome molybdenum: a very hard and strong alloy steel used for pitons and karabiners; developed for climbing purposes by Yvon Chouinard in the USA. Its great advantage is that it is not susceptible to metal fatigue.

*crampons* – a steel framework with ten or twelve spikes, attached to the soles of boots for ice climbing

*direct aid* – artificial climbing

*duvet* (French: 'down') – used to make jackets, trousers and bivouac equipment; also used by itself to mean a down jacket

*étrier* (French: 'stirrup') – used in artificial climbing. Like a short ladder, made either of rope with two to four aluminium rungs, or of a tape sling knotted to form rungs. The climber hangs the étrier from a piton and stands up in it.

*extreme climbing* – the limits of what is physically and psychologically possible

*Fifi hook* – used in artificial climbing. Instead of having to attach his étrier to a piton with a karabiner, the climber hooks it on with a Fifi hook, which is simpler and quicker.

*fixed rope* – rope fastened to a piton and left hanging down a pitch so that other climbers can follow up it, and so that all climbers can retreat more easily if there is an accident or bad weather *to front-point* – to climb ice standing only on the projecting front points of one's crampons, calling for strong calf-muscles and good balance

*Heibler* – clamp used for prusiking, replacing the sling tied round the rope with a prusik knot that was first used

*hero loop* – a small sling fastened round a piton where it enters the rock to reduce the leverage against it; used normally where it is impossible to drive the piton in very far

*ice-dagger* – a sharp steel blade approximately six inches long, used for ice climbing

*ice-screw* – used like a piton for ice climbing, but screwed instead of hammered in and easier to retrieve

*Jumar* – clamp used for prusiking in the same way as a Heibler clamp; easier to use and more reliable, except when the rope is iced up, but also more expensive

*karabiner* – a snap-link with a spring-loaded gate; used for belays and runners. It is clipped on to a sling or piton and the rope is passed through it. Also known as a crab.

*Kletterschuhe* (German: 'climbing shoes') – lightweight climbing boots with thin soles used for delicate summer climbing

*knifeblade* – a piton with a very thin blade

*nail* – piton

*North Wall hammer* – short ice-hammer with a hammer-head instead of an adze-head

*parka* – anorak

*peg* – piton

*pitch* – a section of a climb, limited either by the length of the climbing rope – normally between 100 and 150 feet – or by the availability of belay stances

*piton* – iron, steel or alloy spike of various shapes hammered into a crack in the rock; used to belay from or to hang étriers from. Also nail, peg.

*powder snow* – unconsolidated snow, without a crust on top

*protection* – as he advances the climbing leader passes his rope through slings that he passes round rock spikes or attaches to pitons – the sling is known as a runner. If the leader comes off he will fall only the distance to the runner and the same distance below. If he were unprotected he would fall all the way to the second paying-out of his rope and hit the ground or fall the same distance again.

*prusik* – a method of moving up a fixed rope, using either a pair of slings tied round the rope with a prusik knot or a pair of Jumar or Heibler clamps. The clamps or slings slide up the rope when the climber pushes them but do not slip down again. The climber stands in the knotted slings or in a pair of slings attached to the clamps.

*runner or running belay* – rope or tape sling hung over a spike of rock or attached to a piton, through which the rope is passed to give the leader protection

*sling* – loop of rope or tape between three and six feet in circumference *spindrift* – powder snow blown in the wind or falling in an avalanche

*tape* – nylon webbing between half an inch and three inches wide used to make slings and étriers. Also known as Tiger's Web.

*stance* – a place to belay; anywhere a climber can stand in balance

*tension traverse* – a traverse where the climber keeps himself in balance by using the pull of the rope against him

*tent-sack* – a single lightweight tent used for bivouacs

*traverse* – a horizontal pitch

*water-ice* – ice formed from water rather than from snow

# Glossary of Skiing Terms

*basket* – circular disc near end of ski-pole that stops it from going too far into the snow

*langlauf* – long-distance cross-country skiing

*wedel* – method of descent using a succession of fast, nearly right-angled turns

# About the Authors

**Peter Gillman** is an award-winning author and journalist. He was born in London in 1942 and edited *Isis* while at Oxford. He joined the *Weekend Telegraph* as a feature writer in 1965 and, a climber himself, covered the 1966 Eiger direct for the *Telegraph* group, which sponsored the British–American team. He later spent twelve years as a feature writer and investigative reporter at the *Sunday Times*. He has written numerous books, including *The Wildest Dream*, a biography of George Mallory co-authored with his wife Leni, which won the Boardman Tasker Award for Mountain Literature in 2000. His writing has appeared throughout the national and specialist press, and he has won a record seven awards from the Outdoor Writers and Photographers Guild, some jointly with Leni, including one for their book *Extreme Eiger*, first published in 2015. He was elected chair of the OWPG in 2016. He also works as a trainer in journalism and writing and has presented workshops at the annual Byline journalism festival.

**Dougal Haston** was born in Currie, near Edinburgh, in 1940. He was one of Britain's leading mountaineers and a compelling figure in climbing history. After landmark winter ascents in Scotland, he made attempts on the original 1938 route on the North Face of the Eiger in 1960 and 1962, finally succeeding with Rusty Baillie in 1963, so making the second British ascent. He first climbed with John Harlin in 1964. Following the Eiger direct in 1966, Haston achieved international fame through ascents of Annapurna in 1970 and Everest in 1975, when he and Doug Scott became the first two British climbers to reach the summit. Away from climbing, he was a controversial figure known for his rock-and-roll lifestyle. He was director of the International School of Mountaineering in Leysin, Switzerland from 1967 until his death in 1977 in an avalanche while skiing. The day before his death he had finished writing a novel, *Calculated Risk*, which now appears like a death foretold. It was published in 1979.

**Chris Bonington** – mountaineer, writer, photographer and lecturer – was born in London in 1934. He first climbed in Snowdonia at the age of sixteen and has since become one of the pre-eminent figures in British mountaineering. He made the first British ascent of the North Face of the Eiger by the original route in 1962, and led the expeditions that made the first ascents of the South Face of Annapurna in 1970 and the South-West Face of Everest in 1975. He reached the summit of Everest himself with a Norwegian expedition in 1985. He has written numerous books, fronted television programmes, and lectured to the public and corporate audiences all over the world. He was awarded a knighthood in 1996 for services to mountaineering.

Peter Gillman makes a radio call from Kleine Scheidegg to the climbers on the North Face.

Layton Kor and John Harlin below the Eiger before the attempt.

Dougal Haston rests after descending from the North Face with Harlin on 16 March, following their enforced five-day stay at the Death Bivouac snow cave during a savage storm. Peter Gillman took this shot and the next when he and Chris Bonington met the two climbers after their descent.

119

Harlin below the face on 16 March. He appears to be striking a he-man pose but was in fact pulling on his rucksack.

Kor on 19 March making one of the most crucial leads in the ascent, the traverse at the foot of the Central Pillar that opened up the route to the Spider.

The mountaineering life: Harlin faces Bonington's camera in the Death Bivouac snow-hole, while Kor and Haston snuggle into their down bivouac equipment behind.

The five successful climbers – four German, one Scottish – pose for Bonington on the West Flank during their descent on 26 March, the day after they reached the summit.
*Left to right:* Jörg Lehne, Günther Strobel, Roland Votteler, Dougal Haston, Sigi Hupfauer

WEST
FLANK

| | | |
|---|---|---|
| ☐▭▭▭ DIRECT ROUTE | ① FOOT OF FIXED ROPES | ⑪ KOR TRAVERSE |
| ▭ ▭ ▭ 1938 ROUTE | ② FIRST ICE CAVES | ⑫ RAMP |
| ○○○○○○○ GERMAN LINE WHERE DIFFERENT | ③ FIRST BAND | ⑬ CENTRAL PILLAR |
| | ④ FIRST ICEFIELD | ⑭ ROPE BROKE HERE |
| | ⑤ SECOND BAND | ⑮ TRAVERSE OF THE GODS |
| | ⑥ SECOND ICEFIELD | ⑯ SPIDER |
| | ⑦ FLATIRON | ⑰ FLY |
| | ⑧ DEATH BIVOUAC | ⑱ EXIT CRACKS |
| | ⑨ THIRD ICEFIELD | ⑲ SUMMIT |
| | ⑩ GERMAN FALSE LINE | |

Printed in the USA
CPSIA information can be obtained
at www.ICGtesting.com
JSHW012017140824
68134JS00025B/2460